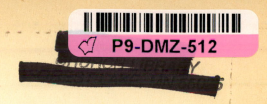

Small Miracles of
Love & Friendship

Also by the authors:

Small Miracles:
Extraordinary Coincidences
from Everyday Life

Small Miracles II:
Heartwarming Gifts of
Extraordinary Coincidences

Small Miracles of Love & Friendship

Remarkable Coincidences of Warmth and Devotion

Yitta Halberstam
&
Judith Leventhal

ADAMS MEDIA CORPORATION
Holbrook, Massachusetts

For Raizy Steg —
In celebration of twenty-one years of friendship.
Your steadfast love, unwavering support,
and exceptional kindness throughout the years
has nourished me, sustained me and helped me grow.
Your friendship is a miracle in my life,
a blessing from God. — YHM

I dedicate this book to those with whom I dance in the inner circle
of love and friendship; Jules, my husband, Arielle and Shira, my little girls,
and my dearest friend Pesi Dinnerstein. — JFL

Published by Adams Media Corporation
260 Center Street, Holbrook, MA 02343

ISBN: 1-58062-180-5

Printed in Canada.

First Edition
J I H G F E D C

Library of Congress Cataloging-in-Publication Data
Mandelbaum, Yitta Halberstam.
Small miracles of love and friendship : remarkable coincidences of warmth
and devotion / by Yitta Halberstam and Judith Leventhal.
p. cm.
ISBN 1-58062-180-5
1. Miracles Case studies. I. Leventhal, Judith. II. Title.
BL 487.M36   1999
291.2'117—dc21   99-32390
                                     CIP

Cover photo Alaska Stock, ©1997 Michael DeYoung.

This book is available at quantity discounts for bulk purchases.
For information, call 1-800-872-5627.

Visit the Adams Media home page at http://www.adamsmedia.com
Visit the Small Miracles home page at http://www.adamsmedia.com/smallmiracles

Introduction

An old story is told about a tough, weather-beaten, leather-skinned Alaskan, morosely nursing drink after drink in a bar in Anchorage. He tells the bartender, with acrimony in his voice, that he has lost the faith he used to have in God.

"I had a terrible accident in the Alaskan wilderness," he confides. "My twin-engine plane went down in the tundra, hundreds of miles away from civilization. I lay pinned in the wreckage for hours, believing that God would somehow help me. I cried out to God, I prayed with every ounce of strength I had left, I begged for rescue. But even as I started freezing to death, God didn't lift a finger to help me. So now I'm done with that charade," the Alaskan concludes bitterly, "and my faith in God is gone."

The bartender squints at the Alaskan in puzzlement. "But I don't understand," he protests. "You're here, alive, telling me the story. Obviously you *were* saved."

"Oh, yeah, that's right," concedes the Alaskan. "Because finally some Eskimo came along . . ."

What we, the authors, are attempting to achieve with our *Small Miracles* series is to heighten awareness about the positive energy, the blessed encounters, the wondrous events that pour into everyone's life! Sadly, sometimes these experiences are misapprehended, or, not even apprehended at all.

Some people, who misidentify these experiences as pure coincidence, dismiss them as "happenstance," "random," or "just plain luck." But we say: There is no such thing as coincidence! There are no accidents! And these events are, in fact, nothing less than "small miracles," awe-inspiring moments that should be celebrated, indeed consecrated, when they brush against us with their soft angel's wings.

These miracles testify to the presence of a Higher Power in our seemingly ordinary lives; these miracles demonstrate the truth that we are all part of a larger organism and interconnected; these miracles illuminate how an invisible Hand is perpetually guiding us, gently prodding us toward our destiny. These miracles make us believe that our lives have purpose, that the events in our lives have purpose, and that we as human beings have hallowed purpose.

And, of all the miracles that we are privileged to witness in our lifetime, there is no greater phenomenon than the all-powerful, transformative, and healing miracle of love.

Indeed, we have all been captivated by media accounts that attest to the power of love and the miracles it can achieve: Mothers suddenly possessed of Herculean strength who lift cars off children pinned underneath; lovers who undaunted walk hundreds of

miles in a Siberian wasteland to find each other;
parents with no medical or scientific background who
discover the cure for their child's rare genetic disease.
How can these things happen? "Life is not a problem to
be solved, "said mythologist Joseph Campbell, "but a
mystery to be experienced."

Love nourishes, comforts, strengthens, sustains.
Love creates invisible lines of connection. Love begets
miracles.

The real-life stories of extraordinary coincidences
contained within this third volume revolve around many
different types of love—love between friends, between
family members, between couples—illuminating the
truth of Antoine Saint-Exupery's oft-quoted observation:
"It is only with the heart that one can see rightly; for
what is essential is invisible to the eye."

A great mystical master, Rabbi Nachman of Bratslov,
once declared:

"Some people tell stories to get other people to go to
sleep; I tell stories in order to get them to wake up!"

This then is our very purpose and mandate in writing
Small Miracles. To create an awareness of the holy and
magical moments in our lives, so that we can receive them
in their fullness when they unfold, with a deepened sense
of gratitude and awe. "Only that day dawns to which we
are awake," said Henry David Thoreau. Seize the Day!
And seize the "small miracles" when they come!

May we all be blessed with the eyes to see the sun rise, the ears to hear the soft morning voices that break out of the silence of the night, and the hearts to open to a new day. Every morning brings a new beginning, the birth of new possibilities, the potential to recreate ourselves. If we are in harmony with the universe, in sync with its cosmic heartbeat, the possibilities expand along with our souls.

As the Indian poet Rumi gently counsels in his beloved poem:

> *The breeze of dawn has secrets to tell you.*
> *Don't go back to sleep.*
> *You must ask for what you really want.*
> *Don't go back to sleep.*
> *People are going back and forth across the doorsill*
> *where the two worlds touch.*
> *The door is round and open*
> *Don't go back to sleep.*

Note: Names followed by an asterisk are pseudonyms.

*S*he was only fifteen and a half when the photographer from the *Chicago Daily News* impulsively snapped her picture.

It was the winter of 1938, and despite the harsh weather and the snow on the ground, she and a group of her friends had decided, in a moment of youthful impetuosity, to visit—of all places—the Chicago Botanic Garden.

Frolicking in the slush with galoshes on their feet and sun in their hair, they made for an engaging portrait. A newspaper photographer was in the garden this day. He was taken by the girls' exuberance, their winsome appeal, and the total delightedness. But he was particularly captivated by one of the young girls—the one with the heart-shaped face, round eyes, and beautiful smile. Somehow, despite the lifelessness of the vegetation all around them, he managed to find a single fresh flower, which he placed in her hands. The next day, a large photo, dominating almost half the newspaper page, appeared on the front cover of the Metro section.

Harry Allswang, twenty-two, was one of the thousands that day who were struck by the incongruity—and symbolism—of that alluring photograph. Here, clearly, was life springing forth from the dormancy of winter. The photographer's message was inspiring to behold.

Even more heartening, however, was the young lady herself. She was, quite simply, beautiful. Harry's heart skipped a beat as he studied the picture intently, over and over again.

I sure would like to meet her, he thought. *I wonder how I could track her down?*

He was entranced, hypnotized, smitten by that young girl. He couldn't quite believe what had happened to him, but it seemed as though he had actually fallen in love with the face in the photograph.

Days after seeing that picture, he felt haunted compelled to hunt for the girl. But after a while, his resolution faltered. "What's the sense of it?" he asked himself. "How could I be in love with a photograph? It's ridiculous!" Soon, the overwhelming need to find her faded, and he put the photo out of his mind.

Years later, Harry enlisted in the U.S. Army, where he served as a machine gun instructor in the Armored Division at Fort Knox, Kentucky. He was now an eligible bachelor of twenty-seven, and many good-hearted people from Louisville, Kentucky, who graciously hosted soldiers' weekend stays in their homes, introduced him to young ladies from the community. But none of them captured his attention.

In 1945, three weeks out of the service and back in Chicago, Harry and a friend were discussing plans to attend a Sunday night singles dance. Their conversation might have been lifted directly from the movie *Marty*.

"I hear there's one at the Morrison Hotel," Harry said. "Let's go there!"

"Hey," said his friend, "what about the one at the Hilton?"

Harry wrinkled his forehead in puzzlement. "One at the Hilton?" he repeated dumbly. "I haven't heard of any dances there. Are you sure?"

"Wherever you want to go, Harry," answered his friend. "It doesn't make any difference to me."

"Nor me," Harry said, indifferently. "Doesn't make any difference to me, either. . . . All right," he chose arbitrarily, "let's go to the Hilton, then. I've never gone to a dance there."

As Harry entered the ballroom, he scanned the throng of hundreds, looking for a familiar face. There was none, but his attention was immediately drawn to one particular young lady, who seemed to stand out from the crowd. She had a certain aura about her, and she was beautiful.

"See that girl?" Harry whispered to his friend. "I'm going to ask her for the first dance."

But by the time he cut across the ballroom and found her, he was too late. She was twirling around in the arms of another partner, who had gotten there first. Harry was disappointed. He asked another girl to dance, but all the while kept his eyes fastened on the first.

Her name was Betty. He got to her side in time for the second dance, and the third, and the fourth, and the fifth, and the sixth. In fact, they danced all night together, and never changed partners once.

By evening's end, they both knew it was just a "beginning."

They felt completely at ease with one another, but it was more than that. There was a sense of familiarity, of recognition, of kinship. A strong sense of this-was-meant-to-be. They couldn't quite explain it, but a certain magic had brushed against them like soft angel's wings.

On the third date, Harry proposed. And it was only after they were engaged that they both discovered just how meant-to-be this relationship really was.

They were taking a walk in the Chicago Botanic Garden one day, marveling at its lush beauty, when Betty started to reminisce.

"You know, about seven years ago," she casually told Harry, "when I was just fifteen and a half, a photographer from the *Chicago Daily News* snapped my picture when I was here with my friends. It was in December. The photo appeared the very next day, and it was quite a thrill for me to find myself on the front cover of the Metro section."

Harry froze. He turned to his fiancée and asked slowly, in shock: "And in the picture . . . did you have galoshes on your feet and a flower in your hand?"

Now it was Betty's turn to be overwhelmed with surprise.

"Why, yes!" she exclaimed. "How could you possibly know?"

"My darling," he answered, "I fell in love with you a long time ago. . . . Let me tell you just how surely we were meant to be. . . ."

And then he told her about the moment their fates were first linked.

Fifty-four years later, eighty-three-year-old Harry and seventy-six-year-old Betty Allswang are still together, still happily married, proving, serendipitously, that sometimes life *is* a fairy tale, and "happily ever after" is just the *beginning,* not the ending, of the story.

Comment
Like magnets we are drawn to people and places that will complete us in some special way.

$\mathcal{I}n$ the early sixties, in an old, ramshackle church located in a small town in upstate New York, a young, idealistic priest valiantly struggles against his church's discouraging state of disrepair and general appearance of genteel poverty.

One morning, when the priest and his wife walk into the building to inspect it after a wild rainstorm has raked the town the previous night, they are concerned that the high gusts may have wreaked serious damage. Their anxiety is well-founded. On the floor they discover an enormous chunk of plaster that has fallen from a wall. Its collapse has left a large, gaping, and very ugly hole.

"Oh, no!" moans the young wife, staring with dismay at the destruction. The rampaging winds have created a massive and hideous crater.

The young priest feels discouraged. How could this catastrophe have occurred on this particular morning—a morning when it will be very difficult, if not impossible, to find workmen to quickly repair the damage? He asks his wife whom she thinks they should call. She gently reminds him that even if they could find someone to do the job, the church coffer is empty. How will they pay?

The priest sighs and shrugs his shoulders. "We'll have to come up with a different plan," he says.

Later that day, he attends a local charity auction where he had promised weeks before to put in an appearance. His mind is on the gaping hole in the wall, but he knows the townspeople are expecting him.

At the event, a beautiful, handmade, gold-and-ivory lace tablecloth is held up by the auctioneer. It is exquisite and eye-catching, but no one wants it because it's oversized. "What size table did that cloth cover, anyway?" someone grumbles in disappointment.

Meanwhile, a creative plan is taking root in the priest's mind. No one else wants the cloth—why not him? He measures the elaborate tablecloth with his eye and determines that it is precisely the right size. It will cover the hideous hole perfectly. He buys it for six dollars and elatedly returns to the church with his prize.

As he turns to enter the building, he pauses. He observes an elderly woman, shivering in the cold, standing at the corner bus stop. She is a stranger to the town. She looks as though she has fallen on hard times, and her coat seems too thin to protect her from the harsh winds. He approaches her and asks if she would like to rest in the church for a while and warm up a little. He knows this particular bus route by heart, and the next bus is not due for another half hour.

The woman eagerly accepts the priest's offer and follows him into the church. As he begins to hang the tablecloth over the gaping hole, she slips into a pew and rests. Then her eyes start to rove over the humble church, and they widen as she observes the priest busy at his task. She seems transfixed by the scene, and she slowly rises and walks toward the wall where the priest is engrossed in his work. Her eyes fill with tears.

"Years ago," she says softly, "I owned a very similar tablecloth. My beloved husband gave it to me with my initials embroidered into the corner. He—and the tablecloth—belonged to a different time. They're both gone now, and my life is so empty without him."

The priest murmurs his compassion, stricken by the woman's sorrowful face.

She advances closer. "It reminds me so much of my old tablecloth," she repeats. "It's remarkably similar."

She walks as if in a trance to the wall and examines the cloth. Mutely, she motions the priest over to her side. There are indeed initials embroidered in the corner.

"*My* initials," she says.

She tells the priest that she was an affluent woman in Vienna, Austria, before World War II. During the course of the war, she lost her entire family and all her possessions. "I don't know how my tablecloth made its way here," she marvels.

The two speculate but cannot come up with any conceivable scenario that makes sense. One of life's little mysteries, they conclude.

The priest asks the woman, a stranger, how she has come to be in the little town today. She says that she's from a neighboring city and traveled to the hamlet to interview for a job as a nanny. She hadn't won the position. "Too old, I suppose," she says, disheartened.

The priest asks her gently if she wants the tablecloth back. Although it was a symbol of her husband's love and the once-splendid life she lived in Vienna, she says, she has no use for it today.

"My dining table is very small now," she says simply. "I am happy that my tablecloth can provide an important function here. Its beauty will enhance your evening service, I'm sure, so I'm happy to donate it."

Later that evening, services are held and the church is overflowing with parishioners. Many comment on the magnificent lace tablecloth hanging on the wall, enchanted by its beauty. Several stop to examine it curiously before hurrying home.

One man seems particularly fascinated, almost hypnotized by the resplendent cloth. He is a "regular," a devoted member of the parish for close to two decades, and he knows the young priest well. He taps him on the shoulder, and the priest, surprised, looks into the man's tear-filled eyes.

"I have never seen a tablecloth like that since," he murmurs.

"Excuse me?" the priest asks, bewildered.

"Years ago, before my life here," the man says slowly, "I led another life, a totally different one. I lived in Vienna before Hitler assumed power, and in the chaos of the war, my entire family vanished. I searched for them for years afterward but was finally told that they were all dead. I couldn't stay in Vienna alone; there were just too many painful memories and ghosts there, so I made my way to America and settled here. I've made a new life for myself, but I never remarried. No one could replace my dear wife. I once gave her a very similar tablecloth—remarkably similar. In fact, I had her initials embroidered in a corner."

Silently, the priest leads the man toward the cloth. The man inspects the corner, and his eyes light up in wonderment and awe.

"It's the very same tablecloth," he exclaims. "It's her initials . . . my beloved wife's! How could this possibly be?"

The priest drapes an arm around the elderly parishioner's shoulder and gently guides him to a pew. In a slow and careful way, the priest tells him about the woman who had been in the church earlier that day. He chides himself for having failed to take her address in the neighboring city, but is grateful that he remembers the family name of the people with whom she had interviewed.

In great excitement, the two men track down the family, who, by great good fortune, have saved her application.

The next day, the man joins his wife, from whom he has been separated since World War II—reunited by a lace tablecloth that had once adorned their lives and has now in fact reconnected them.

Comment
That which love embroiders, neither time nor turmoil can erase.

Rhonda Gill froze as she heard her four-year-old daughter, Desiree, sobbing quietly in the family room of their home. She tiptoed through the door. The little girl was hugging a photograph of her father, who had died nine months earlier after a long illness. As Rhonda watched, Desiree gently ran her fingers around his face. "Daddy," she said softly, "why won't you come back?" Rhonda felt a surge of despair. It had been hard enough coping with Ken's death, but Desiree's grief was more than she could bear. *If only I could tear the pain out of her*, Rhonda thought.

Instead of gradually adjusting to the death of her father, Desiree completely refused to accept it. "I know where Daddy is," she would tell her mother. "He's at work. He'll be home soon." Even when she played with her toy telephone, Desiree pretended she was chatting with him: "I miss you, Daddy," she said. "When will you come back?"

Seven weeks later, after Rhonda had moved from Yuba City, Calif., to her mother Trish's home 16 kilometres away in Live Oak, Desiree was still inconsolable. "I just don't know what to do, Mom," Rhonda told her mother.

One evening the three of them sat outside gazing at the stars. "See that one there, Desiree?" her grandmother said, pointing at a bright speck near the horizon. "That's your daddy shining down from where he lives in heaven." Several nights later Rhonda woke to find Desiree on the doorstep in her pajamas, weeping as she looked for her daddy's star in the sky. Twice Rhonda and her mother took her to a child therapist, but nothing seemed to help.

The grandmother took Desiree to Ken's grave, hoping this would help her come to terms with his death. In the parklike cemetery, the child laid her head against his granite gravestone and said, "Maybe if I listen hard enough, I can hear Daddy talk to me."

Later Rhonda said: "Why don't you write Daddy instead of trying to talk with him? You can leave your letters at the cemetery." Desiree liked the idea, and at home she busied herself on the living-room floor making drawings. Then she asked her mother and grandmother to write out her messages.

When they next visited the gravesite, Desiree tucked her drawings and letters of love amid the flowers. But the following week she saw her messages still lying there. "He's not getting my letters," she sobbed. Rhonda was near her wits' end.

Then one evening as Rhonda tucked her child in, Desiree announced, "I want to die, Mommy, so I can be with Daddy." *God help me,* Rhonda prayed. *What more can I possibly do?* November 8, 1993, would have been Ken's 29th birthday. "How will I send him a birthday card?" Desiree asked her grandmother.

"How about if we tie a letter to a balloon," Trish said, "and send it to Daddy in heaven?" Desiree's eyes lit up.

With Trish driving and the backseat full of flowers for their planned gravesite celebration, the three stopped first at the local Safeway. At the rack where dozens of helium-filled balloons bobbed, Desiree made an instant decision: "That one!" HAPPY BIRTHDAY was emblazoned above a drawing of the Little Mermaid from the Disney film. Father and daughter had often watched it together on video.

It was a beautiful day with a few puffy white clouds and a hint of a breeze rippling the eucalyptus trees as they arranged the birthday flowers on Ken's grave. Desiree dictated a letter to her dad. "Tell him 'Happy birthday. I love you and miss you,'" she rattled off. "'I hope you have a good birthday in heaven since this is your first one with Jesus. I hope you get this and can write me on my birthday in January.'"

Using a fine-tipped pen and her tiniest script, Trish wrote on a torn piece of foolscap, which was then wrapped in a piece of plastic. The letter was tied and sealed at the end of the string. Finally Desiree held the balloon by the note and tossed it aloft.

For almost an hour, they watched the balloon, a shining spot of silver growing ever smaller. "Okay, Desi," Trish finally said, "time to go home." She and Rhonda began to walk slowly away from the grave when they heard Desiree, who had not budged, shout excitedly: "Did you see that? I saw Daddy reach down and take it!" The balloon, still visible just moments earlier, had disappeared. "Now Dad's going to write me back," Desiree declared with utter certainty as she walked past them towards the car.

On a cold, rainy November morning in Prince Edward Island, 32-year-old Wade MacKinnon pulled on his waterproof gear in preparation for a day's duck hunting. Wade, a forest ranger, lived with his wife and three children in Mermaid, a village eight kilometres east of Charlottetown.

At the last minute, instead of taking his pickup down the road to the estuary where he usually hunted, he decided to go to tiny Mermaid Lake, three kilometres from his home.

Leaving his vehicle, he made his way through dripping spruce and pine, and soon emerged into a cranberry bog surrounding the nine hectace lake. There was not a duck to be seen, but in the bushes on the shoreline, something fluttered and caught Wade's eye. Curious, he approached to find a silver balloon snagged in the branches of a thigh-deep bayberry bush. Stamped on one side was a picture of a mermaid. When he untangled the string, he found a soggy piece of paper at the end of it, wrapped in plastic.

At home Wade opened the plastic wrap and removed the wet note, allowing it to dry before unfolding it. When his wife returned from shopping an hour later, he said, "Look at this, Donna." Intrigued, she read the note: "November 8, 1993. Happy birthday, Daddy . . . ." It finished with a mailing address in Live Oak, Calif.

"It's only November 12," Wade exclaimed. "This balloon travelled almost 5,000 kilometres in four days!"

"And look," said Donna, turning the balloon over. "This is a Little Mermaid balloon, and it landed at Mermaid Lake."

"We have to write to Desiree," Wade exclaimed. "Maybe we were chosen to help this little girl." But looking at his wife, he could see she didn't feel the same way. Donna had tears in her eyes and was stepping away from the balloon. "Such a young girl having to deal with death. It's awful."

Wade let the matter rest. He put the note in a drawer and tied the balloon, still buoyant, to the railing of the balcony overlooking their living room. But looking at the balloon made Donna uncomfortable. A few days later, she stuffed it in a closet.

As the weeks went by, she found herself thinking more and more about it. It had flown over the Rocky Mountains and across the Great Lakes. Just a bit farther and it would have landed in the ocean. But it had stopped here, in Mermaid. *Our children are so lucky*, she thought. *They have two healthy parents.* She imagined how their two-year-old daughter, Hailey, would feel if Wade were to die.

Next morning, as Wade was getting ready for work, Donna said to him: "You're right. We have this balloon for a reason. I don't know what it is, but we have to try to help Desiree."

In a Charlottetown bookstore, Donna MacKinnon bought a copy of *The Little Mermaid*. A few days later, just after Christmas, Wade returned home with a birthday card. It read "For a Dear Daughter, Loving Birthday Wishes."

"That's an odd card to send her," Donna mused. "It's her daddy, not us, who's sending her the gift," Wade insisted. "We're doing this for him." After a few more days of talking it over, Donna sat down one morning to write to the little girl. When she finished, she tucked the letter into the birthday card along with the book and took the package to the post office. It was January 3, 1994.

Desiree Gill's fifth birthday came and went quietly with a small party on January 9. Every day since they had released the balloon, Desiree had asked Rhonda, "Do you think Daddy has my balloon yet?" After her party she stopped asking.

Late in the afternoon of January 19, Trish's companion, Wayne, returned home from work after a stop at the post office. "Something here for Desi," he said, handing Trish a square brown manila envelope.

Busy cooking dinner, Trish glanced at the return address, didn't recognize the name and assumed it was a birthday gift for Desiree from someone in Ken's family she didn't know. Rhonda and Desiree had moved back to Yuba City, so Trish decided to hang on to the envelope and deliver it to Rhonda the next day.

As Trish watched television that evening, the thought of the envelope nagged at her. Why would someone send a parcel to this address for Desi? Tearing the package open, she found the card and slipped it out of its envelope. "For a Dear Daughter . . . ." Her heart raced. *Dear God!* she thought, and reached for the telephone. It was after midnight, but she had to tell Rhonda.

When Trish pulled into Rhonda's driveway at 6:45 in the morning, her daughter and granddaughter were already up.

Rhonda and Trish sat Desiree between them on the couch, and Trish said, "Desiree, this is for you," and handed her the envelope. "It's from your daddy."

"I know," said Desiree matter-of-factly. "Grandma, read it to me."

" 'Happy birthday from your daddy.' " Trish began. " 'I guess you must be wondering who we are. Well, it all started in November when my husband, Wade, went duck hunting. Guess what he found? A mermaid balloon that you sent your daddy . . .' " Trish paused. A single tear began to trickle down Desiree's cheek. "There are no stores in heaven, so your daddy wanted someone to do his shopping for him. I think he picked us because we live in a town called Mermaid.' ''

Trish read on: '' 'Your daddy would want you to be happy and not to be sad. He loves you very much and will always be watching over you. Lots of love, the MacKinnons.' ''

When Trish finished reading, she looked at Desiree. "I knew Daddy would find a way not to forget me," the child said. Then she pulled the *Little Mermaid* book from the envelope.

Wiping the tears from her eyes, Trish put her arm around Desiree and began to read. The story was different from the one that Ken had so often read to the child. In that version the Little Mermaid lives happily ever after with the handsome prince. But in the book the MacKinnons sent, the Little Mermaid dies because a wicked witch had taken her mermaid's tail.

As Trish finished reading, she worried that the ending would upset her granddaughter. But Desiree put her hands on her cheeks with delight. "She goes to heaven!" she cried. "That's why Daddy sent me this book. Because the Mermaid goes to heaven just like him!"

In mid-February the MacKinnons received a letter from Rhonda: "On January 19 my prayers were answered and my little girl's dream came true when your parcel arrived," she wrote.

During the next few weeks, the MacKinnons and the Gills often telephoned each other. Then in March Rhonda, Trish, and Desiree flew to Prince Edward Island to meet the MacKinnons. The snow was still on the ground as Wade and his California visitors walked through the forest to see the spot beside the lake where he had found the balloon.

Whenever she wants to talk about her dad, Desiree calls the MacKinnons. A few minutes on the phone soothes her as nothing else can.

"People tell me, 'What a coincidence that your mermaid balloon landed so far away at a place called Mermaid Lake,' " says Rhonda today. "But we know Ken picked the MacKinnons as a way to keep sending his love to Desiree. She understands now where her father has gone. She knows he is with her always."

—*Margo Pheiff*

I grew up in the inner city — the rough streets of a deteriorating Queens, New York, neighborhood. My parents were extremely strict with me when I was a little girl, and I was basically forbidden to explore the immediate area where I lived. My boundaries were circumscribed: I was either in school or at home. I rarely ventured outside. Thus, my opportunities to make friends were severely limited.

Perhaps my parents had grown more flexible, or perhaps the neighborhood had changed. I really don't remember. But by the time I turned twelve, my parents began to allow me to go downstairs and play with the neighborhood kids. It was that summer that I met a boy named Manny.

Manny was constantly playing a game called "off-the-barrel" with the other kids on the block. The game was similar to baseball, but no bat was used. A handball was bounced off a barrel instead. *It looks like a lot of fun,* I thought, as I watched wistfully from the sidelines. Manny — with whom I was still not yet acquainted — must have noticed the longing in my eyes, because he approached me suddenly and invited me to join the game. He was the only one in the group of kids who did that, and I never forgot his kind gesture. From that day on, we spent every afternoon together, playing games, telling stories, sharing our deepest secrets. We bared our souls to one another, and we formed a deep bond. That summer, Manny became my best friend.

When school started in September, my strict parents laid down the rules once again. They insisted that I focus on my academic work and forgo any recreational activities. I was not allowed to play outside during the week. However, this didn't stop the indomitable Manny from seeing me. He would climb up my fire escape and I'd lock my door, joining him outside my window (my parents forbade me to go downstairs, but they never mentioned anything about a fire escape!). We would sit for hours on the fire escape, just talking. How sweet it was to have this kind of friend! I truly loved him, although I did not know it then.

One day, Manny and I got into a huge argument, and I walked off, refusing to talk with him. I was stubborn and full of pride: I refused to take his telephone calls, and I ignored his entreaties when he stood below on the street and shouted my name imploringly. A week after our altercation, peace had still not been declared, and once again, Manny stood under my window, valiantly calling my name. It was raining hard that day, pouring actually, but Manny paid no heed. Persistent and without pride, he stood in the rain, just calling my name over and over again, determined to repair our rift once and for all. His heart was willing, but mine was not. I was inflexible and unyielding. In short, I didn't budge an inch.

Finally, despairing, Manny called up to me: "Sheila, my family is moving . . . we're leaving the block." I didn't believe him for a minute. I was sure this was a desperate ploy to get me to talk to him. How could he be moving all of a sudden when he had never mentioned it to me in conversation before? *Nice try, buddy*, I thought to myself as I slammed the window down hard.

I was absolutely, categorically, irrevocably wrong. When I finally overcame my stubborn pride and went searching for him, I discovered he had been speaking the truth. Manny and his family were gone. No one knew their whereabouts; no one had their phone number. It was as if they had simply vanished without a trace.

I couldn't believe what I had done: I had let my best friend slip away without so much as a good-bye. I never forgave myself for my obstinacy, for my stupid pride. *How could I have let this happen to me . . . to us?* The guilt lasted for years. I prayed for an opportunity to fix things . . . a second chance to at least say good-bye and thank him for being the friend I needed during the most difficult years of my life.

Ten years later, I was married and living in Florida — far from my original home in Queens. I was working as a district administrator of a life insurance company, and many of my job duties required use of the computer that sat on my desk.

One day, I was suddenly seized by an impulse to sign on to America Online. Those who use this service know that when one signs on, it is under a user name, not one's actual name. So I signed on under my user name, and I went into a New York City chat room. I asked if anyone there was by any chance from Queens. Someone replied, "I'm from Queens." So here I had found a person with whom to chat.

"What part of Queens are you from?" I asked.

The person replied, "Astoria."

"What a coincidence! I too am from Astoria!" I replied in excitement. "What is your name?" I asked.

The person replied, "Manny."

Instantly, I was enveloped by the sweet memories of the friend I had once had, but had sadly lost.

"Oh, I knew a Manny once," I wrote, remembering those idyllic times on the fire escape. "By the way, my name is Sheila."

There was a long pause . . . I wondered if the man had signed off without letting me know . . . but then his message finally appeared on the screen.

"I knew a Sheila once," he wrote. "What building did you live in?"

My heart leaped. This must be him!

I could contain myself no longer and wrote: "Is your name by any chance Manny Rivera?"

He wrote back: "OOOOHHHMMYYYGODDDDD!!!"

I couldn't believe it was him, though. *Probably some kid pulling a prank*, I thought. "Stop playing with me!" I wrote. "You're messing with my emotions here!" I chided angrily.

Ignoring my message, he continued: "Sheila, is it really you? I've missed you so much!"

Now irritated, I simply wrote back: "Prove you are who you say you are."

He replied, simply: "How's your fire escape?"

I was in such shock that I accidentally knocked the modem off the table and got disconnected. Fortunately, both of us remembered the other's user name and we were able to locate each other again. We exchanged stories of the divergent paths our lives had taken since childhood and of the different destinies that had unfolded for each of us. He expressed his sincere happiness that I had escaped our shabby neighborhood and was now living in Florida. He, however, was still in Queens. Over the course of time, we had traveled different journeys and changed as a result, yet our childhood memories would always bind us as friends.

It still amazes me. Ten years later . . . 1,200 miles apart . . . millions of people around the world online . . . using fake user names. . . . Our reunion was truly a miracle. Now I could finally close this chapter of my life. The guilt was gone and my prayer was answered.

I had gotten the chance to apologize, thank him, and say good-bye.

—*Sheila MacDonald*

Comment
Our sincere desire to right a wrong can empower us to scale mountains, cross oceans, and create miracles in contemporary times . . . online.

*T*oday, pulse laser treatments are effective in removing facial birthmarks. But years ago, when a baby was born with one, there was little that could be done. Doctors' old protocol was to gently advise anguished parents to "leave it alone." Ironically, "port wine stains" (or PWS as they are commonly known) occur with higher frequency in the female population than in the male, creating that much more psychological havoc for the gender that places a premium on appearance.

Kelly Johnson* was a baby of extraordinary beauty, except for one flaw: the large crimson birthmark that stained the right side of her face. In a sense, she was lucky: the birthmark began right under her eye and stretched to just above her upper lip. Had the birthmark encompassed her eye as well, there would have been serious medical repercussions such as glaucoma or even brain abnormalities. And had it covered her lip, it would have been swollen and deformed. As such, she was fortunate. But her parents stared in horror when she was brought to them in the delivery room.

Kelly was blessed with a sunny temperament, and her parents tried their best to help her lead a normal and active life. She had such an outgoing personality that she had no trouble making friends, who, after the initial

---

* A pseudonym.

shock, seemed to forget about her disfigurement. She adjusted well and was popular.

Everything changed when she entered high school, for it was there that she discovered BOYS.

Boys, alas, were not as merciful or as forgiving as Kelly's female companions. They could readily accept her as a buddy, pal, chum, to be sure, but not as a girlfriend. Her facial birthmark was too pronounced for them to ignore.

Early on, Kelly's doctor had told her parents about Covermark and Dermablend, the two premier camouflage cosmetics that were used to conceal the birthmarks. For special occasions, Kelly's mother had attempted to apply the cosmetic to Kelly's face, but Kelly hated the texture of it: it felt like pasty flour. And, even as a young child, she didn't want to hide her problem. "Either they'll like me for myself, or they won't," she said stubbornly.

Her friends *had* loved her for herself, but boys were a different story altogether.

Kelly's sunny personality dimmed a little more with each passing rejection. Her friends began to whisper secrets about boys and dates. She had no similar confidences to share.

As time wore on, Kelly resolved to make the best of her situation. She focused on her academic work and excelled. She did volunteer work at hospitals and homeless shelters and was a beloved figure wherever she went. And she developed a sharp sense of humor, which concealed her pain and blunted the bitterness she sometimes experienced . . . for she was human, after all.

Kelly graduated from high school, and then from college, and saw her old classmates get married, one by one. It began to be difficult to remain in her hometown, so she moved to New York City, where possibilities beckoned. She got a challenging job, and through a roommate service she found a charming apartment with an easygoing roommate named Sue. Everything was looking up, except . . . for her social life.

By contrast, her roommate's was hectic and whirlwind—phones ringing, doorbells pealing, parties left and right. Kelly always hid in her bedroom when the men came to pick up her friend for a date. Under her cheerful demeanor, she was aching and raw.

"Come meet Joe," Sue would urge, "or Stony . . . or Jimmy . . . or . . . (every night it was someone else)." But she couldn't. And she refused Sue's attempts at introductions. "Maybe he has a friend for you!" Sue would urge. But Kelly knew the truth. The first question any man's friend would ask is: "What does she look like? Is she a babe?" So Kelly never met even one of Sue's long procession of suitors, who came and went, in a continuous, seemingly endless stream.

One evening, Sue dashed into the apartment, breathless.

"Oh, my God," she shrieked to Kelly, as she tumbled in the door, "I am running *so* late! I had a meeting with my boss that just didn't end and I couldn't get up and leave and tell him ' 'Bye, I have a date tonight!' Now, what am I going to do? The guy is coming in ten minutes! Shower, makeup, hair, get dressed . . . I'm never going to finish in time. Kelly, if the doorbell rings, please answer it," and Sue raced into the shower.

"B—But . . ." Kelly started to protest. "You know I feel uncomfortable meeting your dates, Sue!" she shouted at the bathroom door.

"Maybe he'll be late!" Sue yelled back, reassuringly.

"But what if he's on time?" Kelly asked, distressed.

"Kelly, you have no choice, you have to help me out here!" Sue shouted.

"Who *is* he, anyway?" Kelly asked.

"New date, blind date!" Sue said.

Just then, the doorbell rang. "Well, you'll be glad to know that he's prompt," Kelly said ruefully.

"Come on, Kel, help me out here!" Sue begged. "Entertain him, okay?"

"Yeah, great!" Kelly said, as she reluctantly went to answer the door.

He's gonna freak out when I answer the door, seeing my face, thinking I'm Sue. Watch his smile freeze as I open the door, she thought, mortified.

It didn't. His smile remained warm even when his eyes alighted on her face.

"Hi . . . I'm not Sue, I'm Kelly, her roommate," she blurted out right away so he wouldn't flee. "Sue's running a little late, so she asked me to apologize for her and entertain you until she's ready. Can I get you a drink or something?"

Sue is taking her good, sweet time, Kelly thought twenty minutes later, annoyed. *This isn't fair to me, putting me in this situation. I'm enjoying talking to him, and liking him, and realizing what I've been missing out on all these years. It's easier to **flee** from her dates than to **meet** them. I'm never going to do this again for her, never!*

"Hi, Keith, sorry to keep you waiting," Sue said as she finally entered the room. Kelly waited for his face to light up at Sue's beauty. It did. *That's my cue to depart the stage*, she thought wryly.

"Well, you're in good hands now, Keith," she said lightly as she got up to leave. "Have a great time, guys."

"Hey," he said to her, "it was really fun talking to you!"

"Oh, you too," she said politely. And turned around, aching.

The next evening, Sue was still not back from work when the phone rang. It was Keith. *Guess the date was a success*, Kelly thought, when she heard his voice. She hadn't seen Sue in the morning when she arose; she began work an hour earlier.

"Hi," she said, when she recognized his voice. "I'm sorry, but Sue hasn't come home yet."

"That's okay," he said easily, "it isn't Sue whom I called to speak to."

"Ex—Excuse me?" she asked, flustered.

"I called to speak to *you*, Kelly."

"Me? I don't understand. . . . Oh, you want to ask me some things about Sue? Sure, go ahead!"

"No, Kelly," he said gently. "I don't want to talk to you about Sue. I want to talk to you about Kelly."

"I . . . I don't understand," she said.

"Kelly, it's not any kind of betrayal, is it, if a man prefers a first-time blind-date's roommate over the blind date herself?"

"I'm not sure I comprehend," she said, slowly awakening to the truth, hoping against hope that she hadn't heard wrong.

"It's *you* I like, Kelly," he said, "not Sue."

"But didn't you see my birthmark?" she stammered.

"I did," he answered forthrightly. "But I also saw your sweetness, your goodness, your bubbly personality, your sharp intelligence, your spirit. And all those things just make the birthmark rather insignificant to me. . . . So how about a date?" he asked.

Thirty years later, they have five children, four grandchildren, and a very happy marriage.

Sometime during their marriage, pulse laser treatments for port wine stains were introduced into the medical community, and Kelly had hers successfully removed.

But she always remembers, with gratitude and affection, that it wasn't her outward appearance that initially attracted Keith.

It was the beauty of her soul.

*I*t was the thirties in Poland—
the tense prewar years—and
relations between Jews and Gentiles had already
become strained.

But my father—five years old and already an
iconoclast—refused to surrender to the fear and
suspicion that began to envelop his town. Even at five,
he was possessed of a free spirit, and a genuinely loving
one as well, so he continued his friendships with non-
Jewish children, despite the temper of the time.

There was one particular young boy my father was
especially friendly with, and, as all young children are
wont to do, they swapped things. Toys, foreign stamps,
stories, jokes. One day, in an unusual display of
ecumenism, they playfully decided to swap . . . prayers.

"You teach me a Jewish prayer, and I'll teach you a
Christian one," proposed the Polish lad one day. In
their sweet, trusting innocence, both thought it would
be fun. They had no idea how horrified their respective
parents would have been had they learned what their
children planned.

Their repertoires were, understandably, limited, so
they both chose important prayers, cornerstones of their
respective faiths.

"Let's memorize them!" the Polish lad exclaimed.
And so they did.
Ten years passed, and everything changed.

By then, most of the Jews of the *shtetl* had been transported to ghettos or concentration camps or were long dead.

My father, now fifteen and orphaned, was fleeing Europe, disguised as a Gentile, aided by his Germanic facial features and forged documents. So far, he had been successful in eluding the Nazis.

One day, he was on a train when a Nazi soldier boarded his car and demanded to see everyone's papers. He scrutinized every document intently, and seemed satisfied. Then he approached my father. My father handed him his forged documents, which had always passed muster. But for some reason, this particular Nazi was suspicious. He inspected the documents over and over again and regarded my father with narrowed eyes that flashed skepticism. Inside, my father was trembling badly. He was sure the Nazi knew him for the imposter that he was and that he would soon be killed.

Finally, the Nazi turned to him and said with a contemptuous sneer, "So, you are a Christian, my friend? Well, just to prove that you are who you say you are, why don't you recite—right now, here on the spot—such and such Christian prayer that all good Christians know!"

And the soldier smiled in glee, waiting to pounce on his obvious prey.

But somewhere inside my father, a long-buried memory stirred. So he obliged the soldier, reciting the prayer perfectly. The soldier, surprised, let him go, never knowing that the Christian prayer he had asked my father to recite was the only one he knew.

For the prayer that the soldier had demanded my father recite was the same prayer that his little Christian friend had taught him ten years before and insisted that he memorize.

And my father, who had an excellent memory, hadn't forgotten a single word.

My father continued to flee across Europe and made it onto a boat to Palestine. He survived the war and rebuilt his life. And, as one of his enduring legacies, he taught his children to respect all human beings, regardless of race, religion, or creed.

After all, it was the friendship of a young Christian boy that had ultimately saved his life.

— *Yitta Halberstam*

Comment

When friends share their most precious treasures, the universe responds with some of its own.

*F*or over twenty years, John Borgese had not seen his father Pasquele, who still lived in the quaint fishing village of his birth—Amalfi, Italy. In 1966, John had immigrated to America with his new bride Aurora and settled in Glendale, Queens, where they opened a small business. Struggling to keep afloat, John often thought about returning to Italy to visit his elderly father, but he simply couldn't afford the cost of a ticket. "Your father's getting older—you better go soon!" his wife, Aurora, would often urge. "You keep on postponing the trip, and you might regret it one day!" she warned.

In the summer of 1986, a close relative of the Borgeses sent John a videotape of his father, Pasquele. John was shocked to see how thin, wan, and deteriorated his ninety-year-old father looked. When the video ended, Aurora was silent, but from across the room shot John a meaningful look.

"You're right!" he sighed. "I'll borrow the money, if I have to. I want you to come with me, though. How about Christmastime, so we can spend the holidays together?" Aurora nodded her assent. "I'll book the tickets today, and maybe since we're booking so early, we can get a great discount, too," John said. John called a friend who was a travel agent and booked a three-week trip.

"I want to leave New York on December 20 and return January 10, okay?" he instructed him. "This way, we can spend Christmas, New Year's, and small Christmas [January 6] with Dad," he whispered to Aurora, while the agent placed him on hold. "We'll have to close the business, though," he added as an afterthought.

"Now, don't you go changing your mind!" Aurora chastised him.

"We're going to lose a lot of money, Aurora."

"John," she said firmly, "it's now or never!"

Half a year later, they were in Amalfi, and for John in particular, it was both a journey of discovery and a trip laden with sentiment. He spent every day with his ailing father, reminiscing about the past, healing old wounds, asking questions about family history he had never dared pose before, quizzing his father about issues related to ancestry and lineage, even getting his father to feebly draw up some semblance of a family tree. They discussed his mother, long dead, and laughed over ancient-looking photos in the family album. They cried over sad memories, conjured up from the dim recesses of time. John savored every moment, as did his father, Pasquele.

"Hey, Aurora honey," he casually shouted to his wife on Friday morning, January 9, the day before their scheduled flight back to New York. "Maybe it would be a good idea for you to call the airline and confirm the return tickets, okay? "Sure, hon!" she answered in a relaxed and carefree voice as she picked up the phone in the kitchen to comply.

"What?!" John heard her easygoing tone suddenly sharpen in dismay. "Are you sure? How could that be? It's a mistake. . . . It's the travel agent's fault! What do you mean, the flight is completely booked? Well, there has to be something you can do! Just hold on a moment," and then Aurora shrieked: "John! We have a problem.

"John, the airline agent insists that our return flight is booked for *next* week, not tomorrow. Can you get the tickets out of my pocketbook upstairs?" Aurora commanded tersely. "She says we'll see clearly that the return flight was booked for the seventeenth of January and not the tenth as we asked."

"God, Aurora," John said as he tremblingly handed her the tickets. "I never thought of doublechecking the return tickets when I got them from the travel agent, but the woman on the phone is right. We *are* booked for a return flight next week instead of tomorrow!"

"Well, call the travel agent and get him to fix this mess!" Aurora yelled. "The business has been closed down already three weeks. We can't afford to be closed for another week! We've got to get back. The agent made the mistake; let him rectify it."

But, although the agent was appropriately embarrassed and apologetic, he was basically ineffectual.

"I'm so sorry," he babbled in mortification. "I just don't know what to say, John. I feel terrible this happened. I don't know exactly how it happened. In fact, it's never happened before. I must have had a million things going on at the same time. Maybe I wasn't feeling well that day. I swear, John, I don't know how this mistake could have taken place. I wish I could do something, John. But all the flights are booked solid until the following week. Gee, I'm really so sorry about this mix-up, John."

The next day, which was to have been the day the Borgeses would have ordinarily departed Italy, plans were once again thrown off kilter. John and Aurora had decided to make the best of their situation and spend the day shopping in Naples. John's brother, Alberto, who lived downstairs, had promised to come over early in the morning and prepare Pasquele for the day. The Borgeses were anxiously awaiting his arrival, eager to get started, but the characteristically punctual Alberto was uncharacteristically late. In what was a truly rare instance, he had overslept and was now overdue at work. *Could the Borgeses take over his usual morning tasks with Dad?* he panted as he popped upstairs to explain, apologize, and promptly hurtle out the door.

"That's okay, Alberto," John answered the rapidly retreating figure of his brother, trying to hide his disappointment. "Gives me more time with Dad."

John and Aurora lifted Pasquele out of bed and eased him into his sitting chair. As they propped him up and began conversing with him, they were stunned by the realization that Pasquele seemed much more deteriorated than the previous day. They became increasingly alarmed by his pallor and mental disorientation. He seemed dazed, confused, and very weak. "Giovanni," Pasquele cried out to his son, "bring me a piece of paper; I'm getting married!"

Just then, Pasquele began wheezing in a peculiar way. Later, John would describe it as a death-rattle.

"I'm calling a doctor!" John yelled.

As they waited for the doctor to arrive, the Borgeses frantically fanned Pasquele, opened his shirt, and tried to revive him, but it was clear that he was fading. "Giovanni!" Pasquele cried out once, rolling his eyes. And then he died . . . cradled in John's loving arms.

In retelling this story that happened over ten years ago, Aurora Borgese reflects: "If the travel agent hadn't made the mistake and we had left on January 10, John would never have had that last beautiful day with his dad, wouldn't have been there when he died, and in all likelihood would not have been present for the funeral. But because of the mistake, which seemed to us like such a disaster at the time, John was able to bid his father a final and loving farewell, mourn together with his family for the rest of the week, and by his very presence give his grief-stricken brother Alberto comfort and solace. Alberto later told us that he would never have been able to make it through the week, had he been alone.

"My philosophy about certain things in life has changed dramatically since that fateful day. Now, when someone close to me makes a mistake, I don't get hysterical nor do I try to get it undone.

"What's done is done, I think. And, of course I can't help but believe that when an error *is* committed, it must be for a good reason!"

❧

Comment

Mistakes are often the garments in which miracles are cloaked.

*S*haron Harvey was a young African-American producer for an ABC News affiliate in Pittsburgh. Frumma Rosenberg was an articulate, educated orthodox Jewish woman living in the same town. Their paths intersected one day when Sharon was assigned to research a special feature piece for the evening news broadcast show.

Called "Women of the Cloth," the piece was an in-depth exploration of the various ways religious women in Pittsburgh expressed their spirituality. For their focus, producers selected a black baptist minister, an outspoken Catholic nun, a Reform Jewish Rabbi, and Frumma. When the producers had asked people in the Jewish community for a referral to an outstanding orthodox Jewish woman, Frumma's name had repeatedly come up. She was running the local Chabad House at the time (Lubavitch outreach center) and was warmly recommended as an excellent prototype of the contemporary orthodox woman. "Oh, Frumma . . . for sure!" everyone agreed.

It was later winnowed into an eighteen-minute segment, but the original pre-interview between Sharon and Frumma lasted for hours, well into the night. The two enjoyed a great rapport and felt an immediate bond. Frumma was very impressed by the sensitivity of Sharon's questions, her intense religious nature, the beauty of her soul. Sharon was drawn to Frumma's piety, sharp intelligence, and spiritual radiance.

It was love at first sight.

Sharon was not only beautiful, but brilliant, an honors graduate of Georgetown University, a Rhodes Scholar nominee, a violinist, and a track team member. Frumma had had warm relations with other black women before, but she had never quite experienced the affinity, the kinship, that she felt for Sharon. When they parted, finally, it was with a sense of poignance, knowing that they would never see each other again.

One year later, Frumma was at a juice bar in the Pittsburgh airport, on her way to a speaking engagement in Washington, when she spotted, from a distance, none other than Sharon Harvey relaxing in a seat at a nearby gate. Frumma had just bought herself a freshly squeezed orange juice and, impulsively, decided to order another for Sharon. Frumma approached Sharon excitedly, offering the tall foaming glass of juice as a gesture of friendship, and clasped her hand warmly. It was a "joyous reunion" for both, and they sat huddled in the airport for a long time, updating each other on their respective lives, chattering away enthusiastically. Then, their flights were called, and they tore away from each other unwillingly. Once again, both had felt the intense and powerful bond that connected them, a special "soul relationship" that could not be explained in logical terms.

One and a half years later, Frumma—now residing in upstate New York—received a phone call from her twenty-one-year-old son, who was living and working in

New York City. He had some interesting news to share, he said.

He was one of many Jewish "singles" who had been invited to a popular Manhattan Rabbi's home one Friday night for Shabbat (Sabbath) Dinner. There had been many eligible young women present, and, he confided with a laugh, some people had observed that he had "held court" with them. But he couldn't help but notice the glowing presence of a beautiful African-American woman sitting directly across the table from him. Intrigued, he wondered about her.

The very next day, Sabbath day, he noticed her again. She was praying in the same synagogue where he was a regular congregant. He had never seen her there before. In fact, she *had* never been there before. She usually attended another synagogue, on the Upper West Side of Manhattan. But because it was snowing heavily that day, and her synagogue was a forty-five-minute walk from her home, she had decided to opt for Services in a more local place. This was her first time there, she told him later. So, they had bumped into each other twice in less than twenty-four hours. He promptly asked her out for Saturday night, when the Sabbath was over. She accepted.

"So what brought you to Judaism?" he asked her that night, fascinated.

"I'm in the process of converting to Judaism," she told him. "I'm working with an orthodox Jewish Rabbi named Meir Fund, and the conversion is going to be in accordance with the strictest standards of *halacha* (Jewish Law)."

"But what brought you to this path?" he pressed.

"Well," she answered, "I've always been attracted to Judaism, from an early age on. I grew up in Cherry Hill, New Jersey, and there were lots of Jews living in the neighborhood. My father, Ben Harvey, worked as a vice-principal in Philadelphia, and my mother, Barbara, was a top administrator in the Early Childhood Educational Program in the Philadelphia school district. My best friend was Jewish. Growing up, I thought often about converting, but it was only much later that I received an exceptional opportunity to explore Judaism in depth."

"I was working as a news producer in Pittsburgh," she explained, "and I did a feature piece on an orthodox woman. She spent hours talking with me, explaining patiently and eloquently the beauty and meaning of the traditions and rituals. She even went to the trouble to re-enact the *Shabbat* (Sabbath) meal for me, acting it out . . . lighting candles, putting the *challah* (special Sabbath braided bread) on the table, and so on. She really made Judaism come alive for me. This woman made a very strong impression on me, and the encounter with her proved pivotal in my journey. It was a key moment in my life. So, here I am today!"

She paused for a moment, reflecting.

"Hey, you told me you used to live in Pittsburgh," she said. "Maybe you know the woman I interviewed."

"Who was she?" he asked casually.

"Frumma Rosenberg," she said.

"Frumma Rosenberg!" he exclaimed. "Frumma Rosenberg is my mother!"

Sharon Harvey practically fell off her chair.

Frumma was fascinated to learn of Sharon Harvey's spiritual journey and the no-small role she had unknowingly played in shaping it. She had not been aware of Sharon's own personal interest in Judaism and was taken aback to learn that their brief encounter had proven so meaningful. Judaism discourages proselytizing, and Frumma had never dreamed that her extensive answers to Sharon's interview questions would spur her spiritual urgings into the channel of conversion. She was also surprised to learn that not only had Sharon's path originally crossed her own, but that now in the Big Apple, it had intersected with her son's.

"Please send Sharon my warmest regards . . . ," she started to say to him, when he interrupted her excitedly.

"Mom!" he broke in. "There's more. I'm not finished, yet."

"Mom," he said slowly. "Sharon and I are in love."

A year later, they were married.

When Frumma and her husband wrote to a Rabbi in Brooklyn for permission to go ahead with the match (which is standard procedure in all Lubavitch homes), the spiritual leader responded with his blessings and the following note:

The Torah is written in black and white. It is color blind. You have my haskama (permission).

Seven years later, the two are happily married with three magnificent children, and Sharon Harvey is also now known to some as Sara Rosenberg.

What made her traverse the journey from Sharon to Sara?

For many years, Sharon Harvey had been spiritually and intellectually attracted to Judaism. She had grown up in a multicultural world and felt comfortable in making the transition. But when an orthodox Jewish woman named Frumma Rosenberg ran toward her in an anonymous airport with a foaming glass of juice as a gesture of love and friendship, the attraction was deeply enhanced.

For with that one simple act of kindness, Frumma had vividly demonstrated that Sharon would indeed find a home in the religious Jewish community.

But just how close to Frumma's home that would be, neither of them could ever have suspected, in that one shining moment, when their destinies became irrevocably bound.

*T*he gladioli in my garden were in full bloom. On my way to visit my mother in the retirement home, I cut three tall stalks and wrapped them in a damp paper towel and waxed paper. Purple and lush, the flowers would make a beautiful bouquet for her room.

When I reached the home, I passed through the lobby and walked toward Mother's room in the G wing. Suddenly I stopped and turned around and headed down another hall to the nursing unit.

I had no idea why I had changed direction, and I cannot tell you why at the nurses' station I asked to be directed to Mrs. Farmer's room. I only knew Mrs. Farmer as the elderly lady who sat ramrod straight in front of me at church on Sunday mornings, wearing brightly colored hats on her snowy white hair. I hadn't seen her for several months and didn't remember hearing that she was ill.

The door to Mrs. Farmer's room was open. She was lying in bed, her face toward the window, her eyes closed. Her thin, bony arms lay outstretched on the white coverlet.

Mrs. Farmer opened her eyes and turned, not in the least surprised.

"Oh, thank you for remembering my birthday," she exclaimed. Then, gazing at the gladioli bouquet, she added, "That's all I asked for."

I put the flowers in a vase on her bedside table and left quietly. I walked down the hall with a mixed feeling of gratitude and awe.

—*Shirley Wilcox*

Comment

That sudden impulse to go left when we intended to go right may well be the pull of another's prayer.

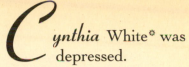

*C*ynthia White* was depressed.

Her movements were slow, clumsy, heavy. An oppressive fog seemed to fill her head, dense and weighty. As hard as she tried, she couldn't seem to shake herself out of the dark gloom in which she was entrapped.

It had been seven months since Frank, her beloved husband of forty years, had passed away, and she was still grieving deeply.

She told herself that she should be grateful for all the happy years they had had together. How many women could claim so many years with their spouses — and all of them contented ones, at that? She told herself that she should go on with her life and try to make the most of the time she had left.

But she couldn't stop mourning Frank.

The fact that Mother's Day was coming—a day that Frank always observed—made her grief that much more intense. He knew how much pleasure she took in occasionally being pampered, and he had always wined and dined her on this day, bombarding her with not one but a profusion of little gifts, selected with love and care.

And always a bouquet. For thirty-nine years, there had consistently been an extravagant floral arrangement delivered to her promptly each Mother's Day morning.

Frank had taught their children well. Although thirty-nine-year-old Tony and thirty-five-year-old AnnMarie lived out of town, they both faithfully sent Mother's Day bouquets to their mother via the FTD service. She had always gotten three, Cynthia mused. Now there would be only two.

Frank's passing had created a deep void within her — a void that no one and nothing else seemed to fill.

If at least I knew there was some kind of life after death, she thought the evening before Mother's Day, *if at least I knew he was here with me in some form, it would be easier to go on. But to think he's just vanished and is gone forever is completely unbearable.*

"Please, Frank," Cynthia cried, "send me a sign that you're here with me!"

The next morning, Mother's Day, the two bouquets that Cynthia was expecting duly arrived. She smiled as two separate FTD delivery vans stopped only seconds apart in front of her house, and she tipped the two delivery men generously.

"Perfect timing!" she smiled as two huge bouquets were hoisted onto her dining room table. "Now how did the kids arrange that?" she chuckled.

She tore open the wrapping of the first floral arrangement and hunted for the card inside.

She knew what to expect. The card attached to AnnMarie's bouquet would be wordy and sentimental. AnnMarie was the more emotional of the two; Tony was the more restrained. His, Cynthia could laughingly predict, would be signed simply: *"Happy Mother's Day. Love, Tony."*

The first bouquet was AnnMarie's.

"Dear Mom," she wrote. *"As time goes by, I love you more and more, and really appreciate you with each passing year. You have always been so giving, loving, and generous. How lucky I am to have a mother like you!"*

Cynthia smiled. Typical AnnMarie. Then she tore the wrapping off the second bouquet. She looked for the card, found it, and froze.

It read: *"Happy Mother's Day. Love, Frank."*
Frank???

Tears streamed down her cheeks as she considered the card. She picked up the phone and called her son, Tony.

"Hi, Mom—Happy Mother's Day! Did you get my bouquet yet?" he asked cheerfully.

"You *did* send me a bouquet, then?" she asked carefully.

"Why, of course, Mom, have I ever forgotten?" he teased. "Would I *dare*? You know Dad taught us well."

"Well, Tony," she asked hesitantly, "how did you sign it?"

"What do you mean, Mom?" he asked, puzzled. "The way I always sign it: '*Happy Mother's Day. Love, Tony.*' "

"Tony," she said, "the card in the bouquet says, '*Happy Mother's Day. Love, Frank.*' "

She heard the sharp intake of his breath over the phone.

"Did you call the order in and tell the florist what to write over the phone?" she asked slowly.

"I always do it over the phone, Mom," he said. "I'm so sorry, Mom," he apologized. "What a shock it must have been for you! The florist obviously made a terrible mistake."

"No, Tony," she said slowly, "I don't think the florist made a mistake at all."

"Mom," he cautioned gently, "please don't be fanciful. I'm going to call the florist right now and find out what happened. I'll call you back soon with this whole matter straightened out."

But when Tony called back, his voice was more puzzled than before.

"Well, the florist checked his records," Tony relayed, "and he did write '*Love, Tony.*' So, then he checked to see if your bouquet and someone else's was switched by mistake—you know, like if there was a delivery to someone living near you with that particular inscription. Mom," Tony sighed, "the florist couldn't find a thing.

He can't figure out what happened. He's freaked out. He has absolutely no idea how '*Love, Frank*' came to be on the card. He's very embarrassed and asked me to apologize, when I told him that 'Frank' was your deceased husband."

"No need for apologies, Tony," Cynthia said softly. "This is actually the most meaningful bouquet I've ever received in my life. "I asked for a sign . . . and that's precisely what I got."

Comment

In the void between what you say and what I hear, the soul whispers its own secret messages.

If there was one thing on which their friends agreed, it was this: Brenda Cowan and Adam Schechter would never get married. They were both practical people, not romantic. Ask them about marriage and they shrugged: Why bother? It's a meaningless ritual.

One night, Brenda and Adam decided to take a stroll. The mood between them was unsettled. Recently, after seven years together, they had split up. The separation was painful, and now they were cautiously experimenting with dating each other again.

They began their stroll downtown in Greenwich Village. It was a hot July night, and the streets of New York City were alive with young couples. Brenda and Adam walked aimlessly, gazing at the shop windows.

They wandered for hours. The pleasure of each other's company was so great, they didn't notice the miles vanishing under their feet. They drifted north through the chaos of Times Square, the crush of opera patrons at Lincoln Center, the crowds of movie-goers thronging on upper Broadway.

At midnight, they meandered onto a deserted boulevard. After so much hubbub, the darkness was eerie. Across the street, one solitary light beckoned.

"Come on, Adam," said Brenda. She pulled him toward the golden light, emanating softly from a tiny shop. Illuminated in the store window was a dress so magnificent they both stared at it, transfixed. It was a simple white dress, gossamer as fairy wings.

"Did you ever see such a beautiful dress?" gasped Brenda.

"You know, Brenda," said Adam, "if you ever wore a dress like that, I'd have to marry you."

A bolt of electricity shot through Brenda. Could this be Adam? The man who always told her that in today's world, marriage doesn't hold water?

"You better watch what you say, Adam," she answered. "I might think you mean it."

At that moment, the shop door swung open. A scrawny old woman, a cigarette dangling from her mouth, impatiently waved them inside. "I understand you're getting married," she said. "Come in."

As if in a dream, they followed her. "Try it on," said the old woman. Brenda stepped into the dress. It fit as perfectly as the slipper had fit Cinderella.

Brenda took off the dress. Still in a trance, they thanked the woman and left.

"So I guess that's it," said Adam. "When should we set the date?"

Somehow the dress had settled everything. They were getting married and that was that. But as they walked along, planning their wedding, Brenda felt her usual practical personality resurfacing.

"Listen, Adam, that dress cost twelve hundred dollars! It doesn't make sense to be so extravagant for something we'll use only once."

"Don't worry," said Adam. "Our daughter will wear it when she gets married."

Again, Brenda stared at him in shock. This was Adam? Her frugal, unromantic Adam?

The next morning, Brenda raced to the dress shop. "I want that dress," she told the two young shop girls.

"Okay," they said. "But try it on first."

"I don't need to," said Brenda. "I was here late last night. The older woman let me in."

"What woman?" The two girls stared at her, amazed. "There's never anybody here at night."

"Well, last night there was," said Brenda. "Around midnight."

"That's impossible," said the girls. "There's no way anyone was here."

"Look," said Brenda, "I'm absolutely positive that—" At that moment, the phone rang. The designer of the dress was calling, the very woman who had let in Brenda and Adam last night.

The conversation that followed was remarkable. It turned out that the old woman, who owned the shop, had not been there in years. She hated the store, and in fact, she was planning on closing it. But the night before, in her downtown shop, she had finished sewing the white dress. And she was so thrilled with her creation that she had felt compelled to rush to her uptown store and display it. Just a few minutes after she had placed it in the window, Brenda and Adam had strolled by.

Brenda was stunned. Was it more than mere chance that had led them to that fateful dress? It almost seemed as if something had been pulling them toward it, something that had pulled the old woman, too. Or was it all just coincidence?

Two months later, Brenda glided up the steps of City Hall, lovely as a princess in her white dress. Striding by her side was a tuxedo-clad Adam. Without a doubt, they were the best-dressed couple getting married in City Hall that day. And as they exchanged their vows, Brenda couldn't help wondering: Without this dress, would we ever have married? Or would we have stayed our practical, unromantic selves forever?

One year later, the topic of the dress came up again. Their friends had gathered to admire their newborn baby, a girl whom Brenda and Adam hoped would someday wear the wedding dress, too.

"You know," said a friend, in between cooing and making faces at their adorable baby, "I still can't get over the fact that you two got married. You just don't seem the type."

"We're not," said Brenda. "It's just that we saw this dress . . ."

—*Peggy Sarlin*

*F*rom childhood on, Nathan Stein always dreamed about becoming a doctor, but it was a dream he had first to defer and then, ultimately to abandon.

Only one year into college, the Depression imposed its stark reality upon his family, as it did upon countless other millions. Forced to quit school and get a job to help support his parents and siblings, Nathan saw his dreams slowly dwindle away. *Maybe one day a child of mine, or at least a child of theirs will be able to become the doctor I never could be, he sighed.*

Decades later, Nathan began to pin his hopes on his grandson, Kevin Ladin, with whom he had an especially warm relationship. "Kevin," he used to repeat over and over again, "I hope you'll become the doctor I always wanted to be." Sadly, when Kevin was only nine years old, Nathan Stein died. But the dreams he had so passionately implanted in Kevin lived on.

For Kevin, like his grandfather, had committed himself at a young age to pursuing the goal Nathan Stein had never been able to achieve in his own lifetime. He wanted to become a physician and heal the sick. And, as time passed, the dream became more entrenched in his mind, being, and soul.

But where to find the money for medical school? When Kevin, twenty-three, was a senior at Pennsylvania State University, he began to apply to various medical schools with a high level of anxiety. How would he pay the first year's medical tuition of fifteen thousand dollars? His parents both worked as real estate brokers, and they stepped up their efforts to bring in more business.

One day, his father, Sherman Ladin, noticed an ad in a local paper placed by an owner trying to sell his own residence.

"Normally, I don't call people who advertise on their own," Sherman Ladin told *The Philadelphia Inquirer*. But, as he explained to the newspaper, he was suddenly seized by an uncontrollable urge to call the number, an urge he couldn't quite explain. It was uncharacteristic of him to pursue business in this manner.

The owners weren't very receptive to his "cold" call, either. They wanted to sell the house themselves and forego a broker's commission. They told Sherman they would wait several days to see what kind of response they got to their ad. If they couldn't sell the house on their own, they'd eventually call him back — they promised.

And they did.

The owners arranged for Sherman to come see the house on a Tuesday. The appointment was formally set and Sherman penciled it into his calendar. But when he told his wife, she exclaimed with surprise: "What? Did you forget we're going to Atlantic City on Tuesday? You have to change the appointment!"

Sherman called the homeowners and a new appointment was rescheduled for Monday afternoon at 3 P.M. "Three o'clock it is then!" he confirmed. But later that day, the homeowners called *him* and said that now *they* had to change the time. The third—and final— appointment was scheduled for Monday morning at 11 A.M.

When Sherman approached the house, whose address he had been given, he experienced a minor shock. "When I walked up to the front door, I realized that this was the same house my in-laws had lived in fifteen years before, and it was a very strange feeling," he recalled.

As Sidney and Dina Toporov, current owners of the house, ushered him into the living room, he began to tell them about the strange coincidence. But he barely had a chance to say a few words when the doorbell rang.

"No, I'm sorry, but there's some mistake," he heard the Toporovs tell the mail carrier at the door who was holding a certified letter in his hand. "There's no one here by that name. We never heard of a Nathan Stein. . . ."

Sherman Ladin jumped up from his chair. "That was *my father-in-law*!" he exclaimed.

Telling the mail carrier that his father-in-law was dead fourteen years, he offered to sign for the registered letter, which just happened to be from a bank.

It was a notice about a dormant account that had never been claimed. A dormant account of Nathan

Stein's that no one—not his wife nor his daughter nor his son-in-law—knew anything about. An account that would be forfeited to the state if it would not be claimed soon. An account that contained fifteen thousand dollars!

"I am sure my father wanted my husband to be in his old house at the exact time that the mailman came with the registered letter," Shirley Ladin, Nathan's daughter, told reporters. "It had to be that way. Can you think of any other reason for that happening?"

Her husband agreed.

"I was put in that house at precisely that time to make sure Kevin would get the money for his first year's medical tuition," Sherman Ladin said.

"My father was always there to make things right for us, and he's still doing it," Shirley Ladin said. "There's no doubt in my mind that my father made this happen and that he's watching us to this day."

*N*o one wants to pull hospital duty on Christmas Eve—or on Christmas Day either, for that matter. To be parted from your loved ones on a holiday, to miss the festivities that are taking place in your absence, is difficult indeed. But what makes the assignment that much more wrenching for hospital staff is watching the pain and suffering of the patients forced to remain in the hospital. The emotional trauma gets compounded when you consider the tragic fate of many of these gravely ill patients: for several, this is the very last holiday in their lives.

Working as I do in a children's hospital, Christmas duty can be both a heartbreaking and heartwarming experience. But when I drew the assignment for both Christmas Eve and Christmas Day, I tried to make the best of it. We hosted a visit by a merry Santa Claus who spread cheer throughout the hospital as he distributed gifts to delighted youngsters, and we stuffed stockings with toys that the patients would wake up to the following morning.

As I and several other Childlife Specialists worked busily in the staff office, someone knocked loudly on the door (we wanted the stockings to be a surprise for the children, so we were vigilant about keeping the door shut). It was a teenage patient who was familiar to us all. He had been in and out of the hospital several times during the past year, and we had grown very fond of him. Despite his own serious condition, he was a very warm and generous-hearted boy. He always took the time to scoop the younger patients up in his arms and give them rides in his wheelchair, read bedtime stories to them, or initiate water-gun fights on the floor, which distracted the children and filled them with glee.

Johnny* had just been readmitted to the hospital that night and had come to our office to offer his help in stuffing the stockings. We were taken aback that this feisty teenager had allowed himself to be admitted—of all times!—on Christmas Eve. Why hadn't he waited until the following morning? we inquired. Didn't he want to stay home with his family and open presents?

A sad expression stole over Johnny's face. "No," he answered, "it would be worse for me to stay home."

He explained that his parents would give him things he didn't care about or particularly need. "They'll give me clothes and CDs and other stuff, and while I appreciate their kindness," he said, "it's not what I want."

"What *do* you want?" we asked, hoping against hope that it was something we had already heaped in one of the stocking stuffers.

"A Nintendo 64," he answered.

Our shoulders sagged in disappointment. It was certainly not among the items we had amassed in our office. We gently reminded him that the Nintendo 64—

the hottest-selling Christmas item that year—was not only difficult to get, but expensive, too.

"I know," he said wistfully. "It's just that I thought if I would get a Nintendo 64, then maybe my brothers would stay home more often and play the games with me, instead of dashing out the door all the time and leaving me alone."

Our hearts broke for Johnny, and if there had been anyplace open at 10 P.M. Christmas Eve, we would have zipped around the hospital collecting money from the staff, hurtled out the door, and bought him one immediately. Needless to say, however, every single store in our neighborhood was closed. When we quit our shift for the night, we returned home with a sad, empty feeling inside. We felt that somehow we had let Johnny down by not being able to fulfill his one—and maybe last—holiday wish.

Christmas morning, my department beeper went off at 6:30 A.M. Surprised, I called in to see what was up, and the secretary in the emergency room said that she was going off duty and wanted to give me a gift that had been dropped off during the night. I told her that I would be in at about eight and asked her to open the wrappings in order to determine whether the gift should be left at Security or remain in ER. She could not fathom why I started sobbing on the phone when she told me that the gift was a Nintendo 64. I have never cried so hard in my whole life.

"How did it get to the emergency room?" I sniffled a few minutes later, when my sobs finally began to subside.

"Some people dropped it off at about 1 A.M.," she said. "They figured the emergency room is open round-the-clock, so it's accessible. They asked us to give it to a patient in the hospital who would enjoy it."

There are no words to describe Johnny's face when he opened that package or his smile as his brothers sat with him in his room for hours playing Nintendo. We were so touched that we shared the story with everyone in the hospital that day. We felt sad that the people who helped make this miracle happen were unaware of the amazing thing they had done. We decided to try to track them down.

I rummaged through the bag in which the Nintendo had been dropped off and found a credit card receipt with a person's name on it. I called information and found a listing for the name. A woman answered the phone, and when I asked if she was the one who had dropped off the Nintendo the previous night, she answered yes. Together, she and her son had stopped at the hospital with the gift.

How had they come to bring a Nintendo 64? I asked casually, noting that it was quite an unusual and expensive gift to donate to a hospital.

"Oh, it's a long story," she said.

"Please tell me," I begged.

"Well," she began, "my son is engaged to a woman who lives in a different state. She has two boys by a previous marriage, and they both wanted a Nintendo 64 for Christmas. Because the toy was so popular, it wasn't readily available in the small town where she lives, so she asked my son to try to get one for her here. He, too, experienced difficulty in obtaining one—it seems to be quite a hot item this year—and he told her on the phone that he had not been successful as yet, but would certainly keep on trying. When he called her a few days ago to announce triumphantly 'Mission accomplished!'—he had finally bought one—she laughed and said she had just bought one too, that very same day! So now he had an extra Nintendo 64 on his hands, which he placed in the car so that he would remember to return it to the store.

"We were returning from services last night when I noticed the Nintendo on his back seat. I asked him what he was planning to do with the extra one, and he said, 'Return it eventually when I get the time.' Just then, we happened to be passing the Children's Hospital so I impulsively said: 'How about donating it to a sick child, instead?'"

I told the woman a little bit about Johnny, the patient who had been the thrilled recipient of her special generosity. She asked me about his illness, and I told her that he had cancer. She started to cry. Then she asked me what type. When I answered, she cried even harder. She told me that she herself had been diagnosed with the same type of cancer the year before, and she had undergone a very rough time with the debilitating treatments.

She had suggested to her son that they donate the Nintendo 64 to the Children's Hospital because of her tremendous empathy for the little patients confined there. If she, as an adult, had had such a hard time, she told her son, imagine how tough it must be for a child.

We used to have a lot of skeptics on staff at the hospital. We now have an inordinate number of brand-new believers, who have witnessed firsthand how wonderfully connected all of us are by the spirit of friendship and love.

And I am very glad, after all, that I drew hospital duty that shift, so that I could witness this wondrous miracle myself.

—Mary Welker

"*Way* leads on to way," observes Robert Frost in his beloved poem "The Road Not Taken," noting how every choice we make in life creates a link in a long and irreversible chain.

In just this manner, two young men living in different parts of the United States, unbeknownst to one another, made a series of separate but simultaneous decisions that altered their destinies forever.

In December 1997, twenty-one-year-old Roger Mansfield and twenty-three-year-old Ron Barren—who did not know each other and had never met before— decided at about the same time that they wanted to move to Michigan. Roger was then living in Washington State and Ron was residing in Florida.

Simultaneously, each one began studying the help-wanted sections that appeared in the Michigan papers, and simultaneously, both noticed an appealing ad for The Greenery—a convalescent home in Howell. Both applied for the same job. Since there were serendipitously *two* openings at the same facility for nurse's assistants, both Roger and Ron were hired. Simultaneously.

Both started working at The Greenery on the exact same day, and both went through orientation together. Then they both decided to enroll in a three-week nurse's assistant class at Washtenaw Community College in order to upgrade their skills and expand their knowledge.

It was at the college that they became well acquainted and took a real shine to one another. It was also at the college that some students began to comment on their remarkable resemblance—but the pair just laughed them off.

In late January 1998, both participated in a class discussion on "Nurturing and Malnutrition," and it was then that Roger shared with the class the information that he himself had been malnourished as a child. He disclosed that he had subsequently been adopted.

Roger had never divulged this information before, and no one in the class could have been more stunned than his new friend Ron, who turned around and said: "I was adopted, too. My last name used to be Fletcher," Ron went on. "What was yours?" he asked Roger.

Now it was Roger's turn to stare in shock at Ron. "I don't know how to say this, but my last name used to be Fletcher, too."

In trading stories, Roger and Ron discovered that both had been adopted nineteen years before through the Children's Aid Society in Michigan. The similarities were too striking to ignore, but before succumbing to the excitement of the natural conclusion—that they were indeed biological brothers—both raced home to ascertain the truth.

By luck, each had in his possession adoption papers that provided physical descriptions of their birth parents and the ages of their siblings. In every respect, the details were identical.

"The possibilities of this actually happening . . . you hear about these things, but you never think they're going to happen to *you*," said Roger.

His adoptive mother, Ronnie Skrycki, said that she was thrilled for her son. "I think these two needed to find each other at this time in their lives," she said.

Considering all the seeming "coincidences" that brought them together, that insight seems just about right.

It was New Year's Eve, 1957 and Lynn was about as excited as a fifteen-year-old girl could get.

Although only a tenth grader, she had just spent an hour talking to one of the twelfth grade "hunks" who went to her high school in suburban New Jersey. He had just asked her if she wanted to go out with him that evening and whether she had a girlfriend for his buddy? Lynn told him "Yes."

When they parted Lynn rushed home to call her friend Irene who lived next door.

"Guess who I talked to?" she teased.

"Who? Who?" pleaded Irene.

"Ben LaTerra! That adorable guy I was telling you about. He wants you and me to go out with him and his friend—tonight!"

Both girls shrieked in delight.

Ben had given Lynn his telephone number and told her to call him with directions to her house when both girls were ready.

"Come over to my house and we'll call him together," said Irene.

But an hour later, Lynn was in despair.

"I can't find the paper with his phone number on it!" she wailed. "What are we going to do?"

Irene wasn't fazed.

"The town's not that big. Let's just call the operator and ask her for the number." This was in the days when all information came from a live operator. Since they didn't know the parent's first names, the operator gave Lynn two possible numbers to call. Unbeknownst to the girls, the operator had given them the numbers for LaTerra and LaTerre without distinguishing between the final "a" and the final "e."

Irene dialed the first number. A male voice answered.

"Is Ben LaTerra there?" asked Irene somewhat hesitantly.

"Just a minute," said Bill LaTerre who had answered the phone. He handed the phone to his friend Ben who just happened to be visiting.

"This is Ben. Who is this?"

Both girls were beyond excitement.

"Oh, you don't know me," said Irene. "You asked my friend Lynn out and you wanted her to bring a girlfriend along. That's me."

"I asked you and your friend out?" Ben's voice sounded uncertain.

Now it was Irene's turn to be baffled. "Don't we have dates with you two tonight? Lynn said we were supposed to call when we were ready."

There was a brief pause on the other end of the line. "Yeah, yeah, of course we want to take you out! Just give us directions and we will come over as soon as we can."

Both girls were so happy. Irene sat in the picture window waiting for Bill and Ben to arrive.

"Lynn! Lynn! They're here and they are both so cute!"

Lynn came running over to the window to look. "Oh no!" she said.

"What's the matter?" asked Irene.

"I have no idea who they are," said Lynn nervously. It was obvious the girls had called the wrong number. "What do we do? We can't go out with boys we don't even know," she said discouraged.

What a dilemma. It was 1956. Not only did the girls feel they couldn't go out with boys they didn't know, they even felt they couldn't invite them into the house. So the four of them spent the holiday evening sitting out on Irene's porch as a light snow fell.

By the end of the visit, it was obvious that the boys didn't care that the girls were two years younger, they wanted to see them again. And so the girlfriends were faced with a momentous decision.

Although both boys were nice, Lynn preferred Bill. But following the code of girlfriends in the fifties, she felt she had to give first choice to her friend.

"Which one do you like better?" asked Lynn nervously.

"I like Bill," said Irene with a smile.

So, although disappointed, that was it. Irene dated Bill, while Lynn dated Ben. But in her heart Lynn always preferred Bill and she thought that Irene was very lucky.

At the end of the next summer the boys graduated and went off to do their military service. The couples promised to write one another faithfully.

But one winter afternoon, Lynn knocked on Irene's windowpane and waved as she walked by Irene's house.

When Irene looked up and saw Lynn, she got a funny look on her face. She went up to the window and held an airmail envelope up to the glass so that Lynn could read the return address. Lynn was shocked to see that it was a letter from her boyfriend addressed to Irene.

Lynn went in the house and said, "I haven't heard from him in two weeks—maybe he mailed you my letter by mistake! Can I read it?"

But Irene told her no, that it was a letter to her and that there was some personal things in it.

Lynn was deeply hurt by the fact that her friend would be exchanging letters with *her* boyfriend and showing it off. That afternoon Lynn wrote a letter of her own—a "Dear John" letter. But even though she was angry, Lynn was too proud to explain and to tell her former boyfriend that she knew about his letter to Irene.

The friendship between Lynn and Irene was never the same again. Although they remained on speaking terms as neighbors, they were never as close as they had been before.

Some years later Bill and Irene married and moved away from New Jersey. They later had a son Glenn.

In 1960 Lynn married Ernie Carangelo. They had their first son Mike five years later. Lynn was pregnant with their second son Don when her life changed dramatically. Ernie was diagnosed with cancer. He died just weeks after the birth of their second son.

So, just 28 years old, Lynn found herself a widow with two young sons. Her husband had not had enough time at the bank to accrue any sizable pension benefits so Lynn was left pretty much on her own.

Shortly after the funeral, Lynn made an important decision. She sold the house, packed up the boys and moved to Florida because she reasoned that it would be easier to raise her sons alone in a warmer climate.

She decided to go to school to study nursing. She made friends with another young girl who was also widowed and who had children. This woman and her kids moved into Lynn's house and they took turns alternating shifts watching the children. This arrangement enabled each woman to care for all the children while the other was at work.

Some years later, Lynn's sister moved next door to Irene's mother. On the first occasion they had to catch up on years of events, Irene's mother shared the news that Irene had died of cancer.

When Lynn's sister called her to tell her the news, Lynn was shocked. She decided for old friendship's sake to make a trip to New Jersey to comfort Irene's mother who was now all alone.

Shortly after she boarded the plane, a man walked up to her.

"Do you remember me?" he asked.

Lynn looked up at him in astonishment. It was Bill LaTerre! He was also on his way to New Jersey to visit his mother-in-law.

They talked as though they had never been apart. It was so good to see Bill again. At the end of the conversation he asked if he could see her again.

Three months later Lynn and Bill were married—over twenty-five years after Lynn had first met him and "secretly" preferred him.

Lynn and her sons moved into the house that had been Bill and Irene's. Bill proved to be a wonderful step-father to Lynn's sons—something they desperately needed since they were too young to remember their own father. And Lynn become "Mom" to Bill's son Glenn. After so much time, things had come full circle.

A couple of years later Lynn was cleaning out the attic which was still filled with Irene's things. Irene had kept just about everything she had ever received.

In a pile of old correspondence, Lynn came across the tattered airmail letter that Lynn's boyfriend had sent Irene all those years ago, the same letter that had caused Lynn to dump him.

Lynn could not contain her curiosity. Her heart was beating fast as she opened the envelope and read the letter.

To her astonishment, it was entirely innocent—just a letter of pure friendship asking Irene how Lynn was doing and saying how much he missed her! Whatever had caused Irene to intimate that there was more to the relationship Lynn will never know.

But now, almost twenty years after their reunion, Bill and Lynn are still happily married and very glad that they found one another again "by chance."

After all, Lynn had always preferred Bill.

—*Bill Cunningham*

Comment
No matter how far it seems to go, a circle always returns to its beginning.

*B*enson was born into a family of loving, doting parents and an adoring older sister. There was little in his life that he lacked, and he grew up relatively content. But sometimes he silently wished that he had an older brother, someone to guide him, teach him the ropes, and—most important of all—take him to a Yankees baseball game!

As he grew older, his yearning for a "Big Brother" increased, and miraculously, he found himself not once, but twice blessed with surrogate siblings. Two older men from the Brooklyn neighborhood in which he lived began to show an avid interest in young Benson and took him in under their wing. Although Jack and Joe were actually friends of Benson's father, they were considerably younger, and therefore able to serve effectively as the "Big Brothers" Benson had longed for. And one day, they fulfilled his most ardent wish, when they announced triumphantly that they had garnered three expensive tickets for a coveted Yankees game.

Benson, they said, *the third ticket's for you. Our treat!*

For a thirteen-year-old boy with stars in his eyes to whom the Yankees baseball team was legendary, a seat in the stadium represented the ultimate thrill in his young lifetime. And, to make the experience even sweeter, the Yankees won that night, too.

It was his first game. And a sports-struck boy always remembers his first game, much like a smitten young woman always remembers her first romance — with nostalgia, poignance and love.

Soon after that watershed event, Benson started high school and somehow his need for "Big Brothers" diminished. The three ultimately drifted apart, and Benson never saw them again. And he never went to another Yankees game, either.

Occasionally, he inquired about Jack and Joe, and learned from the grapevine that Jack had moved to Upstate New York, while Joe resided in Staten Island, one of the outer boroughs of New York City.

Thirty years later, in 1997, Benson was now a middle-aged man living in Brooklyn with a young son of his own. He still vividly remembered the thrill of his first Yankee game, and he decided to replicate the experience for his child. He paid for good seats and saw the same sports-struck-stars dance in his son's eyes when he pulled the tickets out of his pocket.

At the Bronx stadium, they settled into their seats and waited with growing impatience for the game to begin. Benson's son was beside himself with excitement and Benson looked down at his son fondly, recalling the young boy he himself had once been. *Where had the years flown?*

Benson was suddenly overcome by nostalgia for the good old times he used to have with Jack and Joe.

Coming to the Yankees game had summoned up old memories, sweet ones, and he couldn't help but think about the two men who had once played such pivotal roles in his life. *Where were they today,* he wondered, *and what had happened to them?* How kind they had been. Benson was filled with gratitude as he remembered.

He had brought binoculars with him, and as they waited for the game to begin, Benson idly scanned the crowd overflowing the stadium. Suddenly, he stopped short in his tracks, riveted by an arresting sight. *It couldn't be, could it? Not after thirty years? Here? Tonight? Didn't he live in Upstate New York?*

But indeed it was. For there, waving frantically across the stadium (he also had binoculars with him and had also scanned the crowd) was none other than Jack, his former "Big Brother."

After the game was over, Benson valiantly tried to find him, but the stadium had been filled to capacity, and the crowd was too thick. He felt sad that he couldn't locate Jack, but somehow just the momentary encounter across the vast expanse of baseball field seemed miraculous enough.

Since he had promised his son a complete evening out "with all the works," Benson now headed back with his son to a restaurant in Brooklyn that was open late.

And it was outside the eatery that he ran into none other than his second "Big Brother" . . . Joe.

But this time it wasn't a mere glimpse or a momentary encounter. A full-fledged conversation ensued with lots of backslapping, handshaking, and reminiscing, as the two caught up on each other's lives. And once again, Benson felt a surge of emotion charge through him, the same singular feelings he had experienced when he had sighted Jack across the stadium.

Thirty years before, the three of them—Jack, Joe, and Benson—had had an experience that had been etched into eternity.

Thirty years later, when the same experience was replicated, the intricate strands that had been woven into a specific pattern reemerged—as did all three characters who were part of that moment, frozen in time.

❧

Comment

Life is filled with its own instant replays, when the original cast of characters spontaneously reassembles on stage for one last performance.

*I*n 1969, when I was ten years old, I suddenly became stricken with a mysterious disorder of the autoimmune system. First, my knees began to buckle under me, then they began to swell, and finally I couldn't walk anymore. I was rushed to the hospital, where doctors tried to determine what was wrong with me.

My parents had gotten divorced the year before, and I had been inconsolable ever since. As an only child, the divorce hit me particularly hard. Although mind/body medicine was in its infancy at that time, and divorce was certainly not as widespread then as it is today, several practitioners suggested that my illness might have psychological underpinnings. Consequently, I was interviewed not only by dozens of physicians of every stripe of specialty, but by a cadre of psychiatrists and psychologists as well.

Both of my parents were devastated by my mysterious illness. Although I was in my mother's custody, my father asked if he could visit me regularly at the hospital, and she agreed. The divorce had been bitter, but my mother was so grateful for someone with whom to share her burden—both physical and emotional—that she allowed my father liberties she normally would never have acceded to. Only months before their divorce, my parents had relocated from a different town, and neither had yet formed any close relationships or support systems in New York. Also, the two sets of grandparents lived in different cities and were too elderly to travel. Therefore, it was only natural that in their tremendous anguish and need, my divorced parents should turn to one another for help.

They agreed that a united front was vital and set aside their differences for the sake of my recovery. They achieved an uneasy peace and formed a rapprochement of sorts. I was delighted to see them talking to one another civilly for the first time in months.

At the beginning of my illness, my parents took turns at my bedside. My mother would sit with me during the day and then immediately leave the moment my father arrived to take over the "night shift." But after a few weeks, my mother began tarrying a bit after my father's arrival and stopped rushing out the door the minute he made his entrance. Their "shifts" began to overlap, and they began to spend time discussing my case. When my mother conferred with new doctors, she asked my father to be present during the consultation. Once or twice, they even went downstairs to the hospital cafeteria to share a quick bite together. Things got so that when my mother burst into occasional tears—no longer able to restrain or hide her anxiety—my father draped a comforting arm around her.

After three months in the hospital, my case was dismissed, and I returned home in no better shape than before. Doctors told my parents they had not been able to determine the cause of my mysterious disorder and that I probably would never be able to walk again.

Despite this grim prognosis, there was one ray of light in my bleak life: My parents had fallen in love with each other all over again and had decided to remarry! I was overcome with joy.

Six months after their remarriage, I was suddenly able to walk again. I am now thirty-eight years old and haven't experienced any difficulty ever since, except for a slight ache in the knees every now and then.

Doctors were never able to solve the mystery of the strange disorder that had befallen me, nor were they able to explain what caused my miraculous recovery. I, however, have always felt that the entire episode was God-ordained, its purpose clear.

Had I not become seriously ill, my parents would never have gotten together again and remarried. My illness was the spark that reignited their love.

❦

Comment
Sometimes it takes physical illness to restore the heart's ability to heal.

*O*n a cold December morning back in 1956, a thirteen-year-old boy named David, my cousin, huddled close to his mother aboard an elevated train bound for Manhattan. Just one week before, they had left their difficult life in Hungary to start anew in America, in a place called Brooklyn. Adjusting to the overwhelming differences in language and culture, it seemed that they had traded in one hardship for another. But America gave them one precious asset—hope.

David settled into the rattle of the train and pressed his cheek against the cool of the window, marveling at the towering buildings. "Good morning," said an elderly gentleman, jolting him out of his reverie. The man stood before him in a long woolen coat and imposing fur hat. David's eyes drank in every inch of his elegant demeanor. He liked the warm gaze of his eyes most of all.

"Are you new to this country?" The distinguished stranger directed his question to David's father.

"It was just one week ago that we come," he answered.

The stranger leaned over, making sure David felt included as he spoke to his parents. "When I came to America it was in the late 1800s. I was a little boy like you." He met David's eyes. "Back then, I rode on a trolley car. An old man came over to me. He said that he also immigrated to the United States when he was a little boy. He explained to me that back then he didn't have a penny to his name. Then the old man held out a silver dollar and placed it in my hand. He said, 'Here, my boy, this coin brought me great luck in my life. I'm now passing it on to you and hope it will bring you great luck, as it did for me.'"

The stranger leaned his face close to David's and scooped a silver dollar out from his pocket. "This here coin, given to me by that old man, brought me great luck and a prosperous life in many ways. I want you to have it now and as was wished for me, I want to wish that it bring you luck." He opened David's hand and placed the silver dollar firmly on his palm. David closed his hand and held the coin tightly. He knew he would keep it for a long time to come.

The next day, David examined the coin against the morning sunlight seeping through his window. He squinted his eyes to get a better look and then opened them in wide surprise. "This is no ordinary coin," he thought. "It dates all the way back to the 1800s! Yet, it shines like one freshly minted."

Over forty years have passed since that memorable train ride. The small, frightened immigrant boy has grown into a distinguished older man. Happily married for thirty-five years, David and his wife raised four children, all of whom have gone on to raise families of their own. Grateful for his good fortune, David smiles as he watches his grandchildren live with the kind of financial security he missed in his youth. All the wishes bestowed on that long-ago train came to be.

David keeps the precious, silver coin with him always. "One day," he told his wife, "when I am older, I'm going to look for some young boy, clutching onto his mother's coat, gripped by the gnawing fear of living among strangers in a strange country. I'll look for that scared little boy and reassure him, as I had been, that the life ahead of him will bring fulfillment and joy. Just as the silver dollar and those strengthening words of hope were passed on to me and to the kind man before me, I, too, will pass it on."

—Judith Leventhal

*I*n one of his books, the
eminent psychiatrist Carl
Jung relates the following story:

During the Second World War, American soldiers
were stationed on one of the Pacific Islands preparing
for an offensive attack against Japan.

Late one night an American soldier named Johnny
was resting inside his tent, when, inexplicably, he heard
his mother's familiar and beloved voice calling him
urgently: "Johnny! Johnny!"

She sounded frantic.

Johnny chuckled to himself. His own mother was
actually many thousands of miles away in the United
States, and obviously a bored soldier was mischievously
playing a trick on him by imitating his mother's voice.
But who that soldier was and how he had gotten his
mother's voice down so pat, he didn't know. No one on
the base had ever met his mother before; how could
someone mimic her voice so convincingly?

Curious and perplexed, Johnny rose from his cot
and went out into the dark night to find the man who
had pulled the prank.

Johnny expected to find the prankster somewhere
nearby, laughing uproariously, but to his amazement,
there was no one standing around in the immediate
vicinity or the surrounding area.

Johnny was a tenacious sort who didn't easily give up. He also didn't like being duped. So he wandered far away from his tent, determined to track down the perpetrator of the practical joke. But everyone on the base seemed to be sleeping soundly, and no one was up and about.

After his investigations proved fruitless, Johnny finally gave up the hunt and returned to his tent.

But where the tent had stood only minutes before, there now loomed a giant, smoking crater instead.

During Johnny's absence, Japanese mortar shells had landed directly onto the spot where the tent had been situated. All the soldiers inside the tent had been killed instantly. Johnny's life had been saved by the mysterious prankster.

Several months later, Johnny returned to the safe harbor of the United States and the warm embrace of his mother's arms. As he recounted to his mother the dramatic tale of his narrow escape, she shared with him a story of her own.

On that fateful night in the Pacific when Johnny had heard his mother's voice calling him, his mother, asleep in Oklahoma at the exact same time, had had a powerful dream. In the dream, her son's tent was being bombarded by mortar shells. The dream seemed so real she screamed out in her sleep: "Johnny! Johnny!" Her shrieks did not abate until her husband roused her from the nightmare in which she was entrapped.

Her husband tried to calm her—repeating over and over again *it's a dream only a dream*—and her screaming finally stopped.

Mysteriously, the voice of the mother had traveled directly to the ears of her son, thousands of miles away, and saved his life.

Comment

Far louder than anything we can measure are the sound waves transmitted by a mother's love.

$\mathcal{I}t$ was a long flight, and she was grateful when the stewardess finally came down the aisle holding her specially ordered kosher meal. She was starving, and the small midwestern city to which she was flying had no kosher restaurants or shops where she could easily obtain food. She tore open the heavy plastic wrapper that sealed the kosher meal and dug in, ravenous. She was relieved. Lately, during her extensive travels, there had been so many mishaps and mixups revolving around her kosher meals that she was delighted to see that this time at least, she had experienced no trouble at all.

The young man several rows ahead, however, was, alas, not so fortunate. She studied the yarmulke sitting atop his head, indicating that he was an Orthodox Jew like her, and observed him quietly motion to the stewardess after all the meals had been distributed. He asked in a polite, respectful manner about the kosher meal he had ordered, but had not yet, in fact, received.

The stewardess looked down at her clipboard, checked his seat number, his ticket, and then the clipboard again.

"I'm sorry, sir," she apologized, "but I'm afraid your travel agent must have slipped. There was no order placed on your behalf for a kosher meal. I'll be glad to give you a standard airline meal," she offered helpfully.

The young man smiled. It was hard to explain "kosher" to people who were not Jewish, but he tried to explain that he was only allowed by religious law to eat specific foods prepared under the special supervision of rabbinic authorities. In his religion, it would be a major sin to eat anything else.

He would rather starve.

"Can you have fruit?" the stewardess asked. "I think I have some in the galley." The young man indicated his assent, and the stewardess hurried off.

In the seat several aisles behind, the young woman watched the scenario unfold. She had been through this exact situation herself countless times before. She knew how much the young man had probably depended on the kosher meal, and that men, unlike women, rarely packed anything in advance just in case. She gestured to the stewardess.

"Listen," she said. "I have a kosher meal here, and I'll be glad to share it with the man up ahead. Please bring this and this and this to him. Thanks."

The stewardess brought the food over, and the young man turned around gratefully and pantomimed his appreciation. She was happy to have performed a good deed.

At the flight's end, when the passengers began to disembark, she was surprised to find the young man waiting for her at the gate.

"I just wanted to thank you personally," he said. "That was a very nice thing for you to do."

"Oh, it's okay, really," she said. "I am strictly kosher myself, so believe me, I understood what you were going through."

"I'd like to introduce myself," he said. "My name is Jonathan Brand."*

"Hmm," she said, frowning in puzzlement, "your name sounds so familiar to me. . . ."

"What's yours?" he asked.

"Judy Stone,"* she replied.

"I've heard *your* name before, too!" he exclaimed. "But from where?" he wondered aloud.

Then he snapped his fingers. A smile played on his lips. "Oh, I know!" he recalled. "A matchmaker once mentioned your name to me. . . . She said very nice things about you, actually."

"Oh, yes, of course, that's why your name sounds so familiar," Judy laughed, awkwardly. "The matchmaker mentioned your name to me as well!"

There was an uncomfortable silence as the two shifted uneasily. The young man stared down at the floor, embarrassed.

Judy seized the courage to speak first. "I was actually interested in meeting you," she said, "but later, the matchmaker got back to me and said you weren't interested at all. May I ask you why?"

"She mentioned that you're pursuing graduate studies. I told her I didn't want a college girl," he mumbled, flustered.

"Why not?" she asked.

"I didn't think a college girl would be so interested in charity and good works, which is essential to me, my most important priority in life."

"Oh, *really!*" she challenged in a chiding voice. She gazed at him in mock anger, then softened her expression.

"I guess I made a mistake," he apologized.

It's ten years now and the two have been married happily ever since.

❧

Comment

When two souls are meant to unite, even they cannot stand in the way.

All her life, Jane McNally had searched for clues about her mother, hungering for information about the woman who had died when she was only five years old.

She recalled her vaguely: fragments of warm laughter . . . refrains of tender lullabies . . . soft words of loving reassurance still reverberated in her mind, tapping out a dirge of cherished memories. But *vague* wasn't good enough for Jane: she wanted to collect vivid, striking, and intense treasures of her mother's spirit, painted in strong and vibrant colors. Because, the memories were all she had left.

A year after her mother died, Jane's father remarried, and he tried to put this sad chapter in his life behind him. With a new wife at his side, he was uncomfortable about sharing stories that would evoke his first wife's presence; he felt it was cruel and unfair. To compound things, Jane's stepmom seemed especially sensitive—jealous even—of her mother's memory, and the young girl was discouraged from summoning up the past. She grew up with an empty space in her heart.

When Jane married and had children of her own, she could never get rid of that void in her soul. All the joyous occasions in her life—the moments that should have been wonderful and the milestones that should have been heartwarming—were marred by a certain poignancy, tinged by an unutterable regret that her mother wasn't there to witness them.

Throughout the years, Jane continued to hunt relentlessly for fragments of her mother's mosaic, but she seemed to be stonewalled at every turn. The one possession that brought her solace was her mother's wedding album; she leafed through its pages constantly, committing every photo, every scene, every expression to memory. She wondered whether the album couldn't yield up some important clues, and she persisted in asking relatives to help her identify the strangers in the photos. A cousin had once recalled the name of one of the bridesmaids in the photo — Mildred Clabeush — but could provide no information on how to find her.

Years passed, and Jane became a grandmother. She had reconciled herself, finally, to accepting that she would never satiate the longing deep inside her soul. She had pursued her inquiries tenaciously, but nothing had come of them. She was growing older, and she would probably die without knowing who her mother really was.

One day, a salesman plying his wares randomly walked into the tearoom that Jane owned and handed Jane his card. Her heart skipped a beat when she read his name: John Clabeush. She poured out her story about her lifelong search for her mother and asked, her pulse racing wildly, if he by any chance knew a woman named Mildred Clabeush.

"That's my aunt!" John answered.

"It was all such a long time ago . . . ," Jane murmured softly, dread and anticipation both rising up within her. "Is she by any chance . . . still alive?"

"Hey, you're in luck!" John answered jovially. "She happens to be the most spry, lucid ninety-four-year-old I know! Her mind is as sharp as a teenager's! I can give you her address right now!"

Mildred Clabeush couldn't have been more accommodating . . . or more verbose. With a keen memory for detail, she regaled Jane with stories of the youthful escapades of her bright-eyed, energetic mother: on lively hayrides, fun-loving skating parties, giggling-girls' sleep-overs. Finally, a picture of a pert and spirited young woman with an incredible zest for life formed in Jane's mind—the picture she had sought so tirelessly all her life.

After sixty-two years, her heart could finally heal.

During her first visit with Mildred, Jane touched her hand and felt incredible warmth radiate from her being. But it was not only Mildred's love that enveloped her; she felt her mother's presence surround her in a palpable way, too.

Jane has had many visits with Mildred since that first time, and the experience is always the same.

"Talking to her, hearing her stories, and holding her hand is like touching my long-lost mother—and it's finally brought me the peace I searched for all this time."

❦

Comment

There may be many twists and bends along the way, but all roads eventually lead home.

My father was a gruff man. I couldn't remember the last time he had tenderly stroked my cheek, tousled my hair, or used a term of endearment when calling my name. His diabetes had given him a short temper, and he screamed a lot. I was envious when I saw other fathers plant gentle kisses on their daughters' foreheads or impulsively give them a big bear hug. I knew that he loved me and that his love was deep. He just didn't know how to express it.

So, I receded, too. It was hard to say "I love you" to someone who didn't say it back. After so many disappointing times when I would flinch from his sharp rebuff, I began to withdraw my own warm displays of affection. I stopped reaching out to hug or kiss him. At first this act of self-restraint was conscious. Later it would become automatic, and finally it was ingrained.

The love between us ran strong, but silent.

One rare evening out, when my mother had successfully coaxed my usually asocial father to join us for a night on the town, we were sitting in an elegant restaurant that boasted a small but lively band. When it struck up a familiar waltz tune, I glanced at my father. He suddenly appeared small and shrunken to me, not powerful and intimidating as I had always perceived him. Something about the way he looked gave me pause.

All the old hurts still welled up inside, but I decided to dare one last time.

"Dad! You know, I've never ever danced with you. Even when I was a little girl, I begged you, but you never wanted to! How about right now?"

I waited for the usual brusque reply that would once again slice my heart into ribbons. But instead, he considered me thoughtfully, and then a surprising twinkle appeared in his eye.

"I have been remiss in my duties as a father, then," he uncharacteristically joked. "Let's hit the floor, and I'll show you just what kind of moves an old geezer like me still can make!"

My father took me in his arms. Since earliest childhood, I hadn't been enfolded in his embrace. I felt overcome by emotion.

As we danced, I looked up at my father intently, but he avoided my gaze. His eyes swept the dance floor, the other diners, the members of the band. His scrutiny took in everyone and everything but me. I felt that he must already be regretting his decision to join me for a dance; he seemed uncomfortable being physically close to me.

"Dad!" I finally whispered, tears in my eyes. "Why is it so hard for you to *look* at me?"

At last his eyes dropped to my face and he studied me intently. "Because I love you so much," he whispered back. "Because I love you."

I was struck dumb by his response. It wasn't what I had anticipated. But it was, of course, exactly what I needed to hear.

His own eyes were misty and he was blinking.

I had always known that he loved me; I just hadn't understood that his vast emotion had frightened him and made him mute. His taciturn manner hid the deep emotions flowing inside.

"I love you, too, Dad," I whispered back softly.

He stumbled over the next few words. "I—I'm sorry that I'm not demonstrative," he said. "I realize that I don't show what I feel. My parents never hugged or kissed me, and I guess I learned how not to from them. It's—it's . . . hard for me. I'm probably too old to change my ways now, but just know how much I love you."

"Okay," I smiled.

When the dance ended, I brought Dad back to Mom waiting at the table and excused myself to the ladies' room. I was gone just a few minutes, but during my absence, everything changed.

There were screams and shouts and scrapings of chairs as I made my way back across the room. I wondered what the commotion was all about. As I approached the table, I saw it was all about Dad.

He was slumped in his chair, ashen gray.

A doctor in the restaurant rushed over to administer CPR, and an ambulance was called, but it was really all too late.

He was gone. Instantly, they said.

What had suddenly made me—after so many years of steeling myself against his constant rejection—ask him to dance? What had made him accept? Where had those impulses come from? And why *now?*

In the restaurant that night, all I saw was his slumped body and ashen face, surrounded by solemn diners and grim-faced paramedics.

But it's a totally different scene that I remember now.

I remember our waltz on the dance floor and his sudden urgent confession to me. I remember him saying "I love you" and my saying it back.

And as I remember this scene, somehow, incongruously the words of an old Donna Summer song tap out a refrain in my mind:

Last dance . . . last chance . . . for love

It was indeed the first, last, and *only* dance that I ever had with my father. What a blessing that we had the chance to say—before it was too late—the three words that live on forever, long after we are gone, stretching into eternity.

—*Tracy Anderson*

❦

Comment

Just before the sparks of life are extinguished from a candle, the flame dances. It sends a wistful, thin smoke line up into the air, where it circles and pirouettes before it vanishes toward the sky. Light a candle and watch that dance, learn about life and its last breaths.

Everybody in the family noticed the special bond between Nana Rizzo and her two-year-old granddaughter, Andrea. The two of them could sit happily on the floor together for hours, laughing and playing, lost in their private world of make-believe. And when playtime was over, and Andrea climbed on Nana's lap to kiss her goodnight, everyone marveled at how much they looked alike.

On Father's Day, Nana Rizzo came for a family barbecue. The day passed pleasantly. The grown-ups chatted, while Andrea and her cousins ran around the backyard. When night fell, the older children went inside. The grown-ups lingered on their lawn chairs, enjoying their conversation as Andrea played nearby, drawing with chalk.

Nobody noticed Andrea on her hands and knees, leaning over the pool to dip in her chalk. Nobody heard Andrea fall in. Nobody saw Andrea lose consciousness as she drowned.

Suddenly, Nana let out a scream. "Andrea's in the pool!"

In a flash, Andrea's mother, Barbara, was in the water, pulling her out. Andrea was not breathing. Her skin was blue. Her little body was limp and still.

Pandemonium broke out. Everyone began shrieking, crying, running around frantically. Barbara leaned over her daughter and desperately breathed into her mouth, performing CPR. But it was no use. Andrea was lifeless. Nothing they did could bring her back.

Nana Rizzo closed her eyes and whispered a prayer. "Dear God, I'm an old woman. Take me, not her."

In the next backyard, Sam Callahan listened to the shrieks coming from the other side of the fence, puzzled. Was that the sound of a wild party or was something wrong? He didn't live here; he didn't know these people. He was just stopping in for a quick Father's Day visit to his dad.

"Well, I might as well check it out," he thought.

As soon as he saw the terrified family bending over a lifeless child, he sprang into action.

"Did you do the Heimlich maneuver?" he asked Barbara.

When she answered no, he grabbed Andrea from behind and gently squeezed below her ribs. A stream of water gushed from her mouth. Quickly, Sam gave her two breaths.

Andrea's eyes fluttered open. The color flooded back to her cheeks and she began to cry.

"Mommy! I fell in the pool!"

Everyone started sobbing again, this time for joy. Nana Rizzo kissed the top of Andrea's head, then looked up at the sky.

"Thank you, God," she whispered. "Thank you for answering my prayer."

Still holding Andrea tight, Barbara turned to the stranger who had saved her child.

"You're my guardian angel! How can I ever repay you?"

Sam shook his head. "You don't have to repay me."

"But how did you know what to do?" asked Barbara.

"Oh, I was a lifeguard for many years. I'm just thrilled I happened to be here."

In the days that followed, life quickly returned to normal. Andrea suffered no damage from her terrible ordeal and was soon as playful as ever. Barbara, while deeply shaken, found herself drawn back into the usual rushed routine of work and errands and constant never-ending motion.

Only one person did not return to normal . . . Nana Rizzo.

For her whole life, she had enjoyed robust good health. Now, mysteriously, she began to fade away. Her energy deserted her; pain kept her up at night.

When Barbara took Nana to the doctor, he privately confirmed her worst fears. Nana had cancer. The end would be swift and soon. And it would be unbearably painful.

As Nana's health rapidly deteriorated, the family grew frantic. No one could stand the thought of the suffering she would soon endure. Yet Nana remained strangely calm, even serene.

"Don't worry," she said. "God has answered my prayers."

On August twenty-fifth, two months from the day that she asked God to take her life and spare Andrea's, Nana Rizzo died peacefully.

A short while later, Andrea woke up, crying. Barbara ran to her room and scooped her into her arms.

"What's wrong, Andrea?"

"Mommy, I keep dreaming I'm in the pool."

"And I get you out, right, Andrea?" said Barbara.

"No, Mommy. In my dreams, it's Nana Rizzo who lifts me up."

—Peggy Sarlin

Several years ago Diana was a high-powered newswoman reporting on medical news for her Miami affiliate. Because of her public exposure and the expertise she demonstrated on TV, she was constantly receiving requests from viewers, asking her for many different forms of help. As much as she would have liked to, she knew it was impossible to respond to them all. If she had, her life would have simply spun out of control.

But one day, she got a request from a viewer that touched her heart. Mary L.'s husband, Carl, had contracted a rare form of cancerous tumor called a lyposarcoma in his upper thigh. His doctor had told him that the only way to eliminate this type of cancer was to amputate the leg. Mary L. did not know Diana personally—she had only seen her on TV—but she contacted her in desperation, hoping that Diana might be able to provide them with some other option.

Diana felt moved by Mary's plea and decided to help her. But what could she possibly do? She racked her brain. Who did she know who might possibly be able to help her? Then she suddenly remembered interviewing a doctor several months before about certain new medical procedures. Maybe he might know of someone.

"I can help this man!" exclaimed the doctor, after she told him the tale of Mary's husband. "I myself am a specialist in this area! Mr. L. may not need his leg to be amputated after all. There are some new up-to-date ways of treating this kind of tumor other than amputation. Send him to me!"

Carl did indeed go through surgery—but not to remove his leg, only the tumor. It was followed by therapy and the complete disappearance of his cancer. Diana's referral had helped save Carl's leg if not his life.

Mary L. was overjoyed. She wrote Diana a heartfelt card expressing her thanks. It was so beautiful that Diana put it in a "Memento" box where she saved special items. But she never looked at it again.

Almost six years later, Diana was going through a box that contained some possessions of her late father (who had died several years before) when she came across the card expressing Mary and Carl's gratitude.

"That's strange!" she whistled. "How on earth did this card ever get here among Dad's things?"

Out of curiosity, Diana re-read the note. It was then that alarm bells began to go off in her head. For weeks, she had noticed—then dismissed—a strange swelling on her left thigh.

She had assumed that she had pulled a muscle while running, and had waited for it to heal by itself. But the swelling never receded. Diana kept on telling herself that she should probably go to a doctor, but because of her busy schedule, had kept putting it off.

Now, reading Mary L.'s card of thanks, Diana's heart began to beat fast. It wasn't possible, was it? But she seemed to have the exact same symptoms as Carl L.!

The probability that anything like Carl's tumor would happen to her was extremely unlikely—it is an extremely rare form of cancer to begin with—but still, the note provided the impetus she needed. Diana called and made an appointment with her doctor. The first appointment led to a second one with a specialist and then another. The final unbelievable diagnosis: Diana also had a lyposarcoma on her upper thigh!

"You're extremely lucky," the doctors said. "This type of tumor is relatively rare and often goes undetected until it is very large." They reassured her that finding it so early dramatically increased her prospects for complete recovery.

The next months were a whirlwind as Diana underwent several weeks of radiation treatment to shrink the tumor and then surgery to remove it. Those events were followed by more months of physiotherapy and follow-up testing before things began to return to normal in her life.

Naturally, Diana remembered with gratitude the key role that Mary's card had played in leading her to seek medical help as early as she did. She wanted to write Mary to tell her what a difference the card had made in her own life. But she couldn't find it. No matter where she looked, the card had disappeared again.

Diana's many other work and family responsibilities again absorbed her as her life returned to its normal hectic pace. Her older daughter Gillian had had the first two of three shots in the series normally given to school age children to prevent Hepatitis B.

Although Gillian was always sensitive to shots, these particular ones are required by the schools so Diana arranged for them. In the chaos of her own problems, Diana had not yet made the appointment for the third shot and was determined to do so.

Before she could place the call, however, Diana once again discovered Mary's note. This time it appeared in a file containing receipts. Why or how it had ended up there was a mystery. Diana was baffled by how the card just kept popping up in all the wrong places. But she took it as a sign and decided to call the phone number included on the card immediately. She had no idea if, after so many years, Mary and her husband even lived in the same place or had the same phone number.

But they did. Mary picked up the phone and was most surprised to hear Diana introduce herself. "How did you find me?" asked Mary.

"Do you remember writing me a thank you card?" Diana replied.

"Why of course I do." She was still grateful to Diana for her part in saving her husband's leg.

"Well, Mary, you're not going to believe this," said Diana as she proceeded to tell Mary the story of the role that Mary's card had played in her own encounter with cancer. By the end of the conversation both women were in tears and overjoyed at the mysterious and miraculous way Mary's card had changed Diana's life.

"But it's so ironic that you're calling today," said Mary, "just when my own son is about to be on TV."

She told Diana that her twenty-three year-old son, a fireman, had had a series of sicknesses brought on by a reaction to the third shot in the hepatitis B vaccine series. He had been so sick and through so much frustration with his medical plan that a TV station was coming to the house that very day to do a story on his plight.

"The third shot?" asked Diana. Again she felt her blood run cold—the very shot she had been about to set up for her sensitive daughter.

"Mary," said Diana, "you may very well have saved someone in my family a second time."

Needless to say, Diana's daughter has never had her third shot. And both mother and daughter are in the best of health.

And, if Mary's thank you card should ever disappear again, Diana is confident that it will surface just when it is needed most!

—*Bill Cunningham*

❧

Comment

The Cosmic Lost and Found operates according to its own very special system of disappearance and retrieval.

In 1985, I was working as a manufacturer's representative, and in this capacity, traveled to New York City to attend a trade show.

While visiting one of the showrooms whose line of products I represented, I happened to meet another manufacturer by the name of Mark Fisher who designed and sold crystal lamps. We got to talking and, impressed by my professional experience, Mark asked if I would represent his line of lamps in my Ohio territory.

This momentary, spontaneous encounter inaugurated our long-term professional relationship, which spanned many years.

During the course of our working relationship, Mark and I spoke periodically, mostly confining the conversation to professional matters, but occasionally digressing to more personal concerns. At one point, Mark confided that his wife had been diagnosed with breast cancer, but that it had been caught in time and everything was okay. I was sorry to hear the news, but happy to learn that she was in remission.

Four years later, I was no longer able to sell Mark's lamps successfully, so I resigned. I had enjoyed working with him, but it was no longer profitable for me to continue representing his line. I felt a sense of loss parting ways with Mark. I had admired him very much.

I was single at the time, and always thought that I would like to marry a man very much like Mark.

I eventually did get married, but, tragically, not for long. Only six short months after our wedding day, my husband had his first heart attack.

It was at just about this time that I received an unexpected phone call from Mark, with whom I hadn't spoken in two years. He wanted to know what was up with me professionally and also to share some devastating news: His wife's cancer had recurred. I, in turn, told Mark that my husband was recuperating from a serious heart attack. We commiserated with one another and wished each other well.

On May 30, 1993, my husband had a second heart attack at home. He was rushed to the hospital, where he died an hour later. I was absolutely shattered, numb with shock. I knew he had been sick, but I never expected him to die. The succeeding weeks went by in a blur, and I leaned heavily on my friends and family for support. Without their moral and physical help, I surely couldn't have survived this ordeal.

One day, I received a message to call Mark Fisher about a new job. I wasn't inclined to call back at first, but, ironically, the very person who had originally introduced us years ago in the New York showroom called me at the exact same time. I remarked to the caller what a coincidence it was that I had just received a phone message from Mark as well, but added that I was planning to ignore it. The caller, however, who thought I needed cheering up, urged me to reconsider and return the call, which I finally did, in a halfhearted way.

"How are you?" Mark asked.

"Not good," I answered. "There's been a tragedy in my life."

"What's wrong?" Mark demanded urgently.

"My husband just died," I said.

There was silence, and then Mark said, "Are you sitting down? I have some awful news myself."

His wife had died of cancer on May 2, just four weeks before my husband passed away. It was now my turn to be silent; I didn't know what to say.

"Look," Mark said, "I'm at a new job and not really free to talk. Can I call you tonight?"

Well, to make a long story short, he called that night, and every night thereafter for a month.

We talked about a lot of things, especially the heartbreak of watching someone die slowly day by day, and the other extreme of its happening so suddenly. We were able to talk about feelings that we both shared and that only two people who had gone through a loss like this could understand completely.

After countless phone calls, we finally decided to meet at a spot halfway between New York and Ohio.

Our first meeting—within an entirely new and different context—went extremely well.

Six months later we bought a condo, and we got married in our new home.

Who knew that in 1985 I was meeting my future husband?

The angels took us on a long, hard course, but we finally found each other. We mourn our spouses, of course, but my husband and I feel blessed that we have been given this second chance at love.

—Nicole Fisher

*K*evin Chapman* noticed her right away, as he waited for the train at Penn Station in New York. "Now *there's* an attractive woman," he thought.

It was the fifth of July, and crowds of people were returning from the holiday weekend. Boarding the train, he searched three cars, unable to find an empty seat. In the last car, he saw the attractive woman standing in the back. He joined her, pleased with his good fortune, and they began to chat.

She turned out to be as intelligent as she was pretty. Kevin enjoyed their conversation immensely. When the train reached Philadelphia, Kevin wished her a safe trip to Baltimore and got off.

As soon as the train pulled away, Kevin let out a howl of frustration.

"Idiot!" he said to himself. "Why didn't you get her phone number?" In a rage, he kicked over his luggage. He pounded his fist into his palm and called himself every name in the book.

"There's only one thing to do," he vowed. "I'm going to find her. And I'm not going to stop looking until I do."

But where to begin? He knew only three things about her: Her name was Rita. She worked for a law firm. And she lived within walking distance of the Baltimore train station.

The next day, Kevin raced to the library and wrote down the name of every law firm in Baltimore. The list was surprisingly long. Undeterred, Kevin launched his attack. Whenever his boss wasn't looking, he sneaked in another phone call to a Baltimore law firm and asked for Rita. But the pace was slow—maddeningly, unbearably slow—for a man in love. Kevin began to call in sick, spending his days at home, doggedly calling one Baltimore law firm after another.

Kevin's friends grew worried. Clearly, the man was obsessed. He phoned them at all hours, day and night, endlessly rambling on about Rita. The rest of the world seemed to fall away. All he wanted to do was rhapsodize about his beloved and dream up ever-wilder schemes to find her . . .

How about placing a giant ad in the Baltimore papers? How about moving to Baltimore and walking the streets day and night, searching? How about . . .

"Look, Kevin," said his friend Arthur, "this is crazy. You can't go on this way. There are other women, you know."

"Not for me," said Kevin. "If you'd only met Rita, if you'd only seen how incredible she . . . "

"Okay," sighed Arthur. "Tell me the story again from the top. Maybe somehow, we'll come up with another clue."

Once again, Kevin launched into his well-practiced tale. Suddenly, he stopped. "I just remembered something! She said she'd gone to a small college in California!"

"Now we're getting somewhere," Arthur said.

They mulled over this new fact. On the one hand, here was a potentially valuable piece of information. On the other hand, there were probably dozens of small colleges in California—maybe even hundreds. Neither Kevin or Arthur had ever been to California or knew anything about its schools. The chances of their somehow managing to pinpoint the very college that Rita had attended were preposterously small. But Kevin was in such despair that Arthur decided to make a suggestion, absurd though it was.

"Look, Kevin, last night I went to the theater. There was an actress I really liked, so I looked her up in the playbill. And I just happened to notice that she began acting at a small college in California. Why don't we start with that one?" he said, happy that he still remembered the college's name.

In his frenzy to find Rita, Kevin was willing to try anything, no matter how foolish it seemed. He picked up the phone and called the alumni department of the college his friend had mentioned.

"I'm trying to locate a Rita," he said. "I don't know her last name, but she must have graduated about four years ago." He gave a brief physical description.

"What do you want her for?" the clerk demanded suspiciously.

Flustered by the clerk's obvious hostility, Kevin stammered out a garbled story about finding a ring . . . some kind of engagement ring that he overheard somebody say belonged to her. But even as he told it, he could hear how false his story sounded.

The clerk was not encouraging, although he did take Kevin's phone number. When Kevin hung up, he was sure his cause was doomed. But an hour later, the clerk called back.

"We do have a Rita who graduated five years ago," he said. "And her yearbook picture does match your description. But I'm not at liberty to give out any information about her."

"Please," Kevin begged.

"I'm sorry. It's against the rules," the clerk said coldly.

All day long, Kevin blazed with wild emotions, madly careening between furious frustration and ecstatic hope. Could this really be his Rita? Could he actually have found her on his very first try? Was it possible the impossible had fallen in his lap?

At one o'clock in the morning, he dialed Arthur.

"Do you think it's her?" he demanded, the instant he heard Arthur's voice.

"Yeah, sure, why not," Arthur mumbled groggily. "What time is it?"

"But *why* do you think it's her? Just because you happened to go to some show and see some actress who happened to go to some school? What are the chances of that?"

"Look, Kevin. Just thank your lucky stars her parents named her Rita. Imagine trying to find a Susan or a Debbie. . . . She's a Rita of the right age and the right look at a small school in California. Now let me get some sleep."

At six in the morning, Kevin dialed Arthur again. "But if it is her, how am I going to get past the clerk?"

"You'll figure it out," said Arthur, and hung up.

At nine in the morning, California time, Kevin called the alumni office. When the same clerk answered, Kevin hung up. He called the next day and the next, hanging up each time the clerk answered.

But the day after that, a new voice answered the phone—a woman's voice. She sounded friendly, and Kevin threw himself on her mercy. "Please help me. I've fallen desperately in love with someone I met on a train to Baltimore. I think she may have gone to your school. Please, please—can you get me her number?"

The clerk was sympathetic. "No promises," she said warmly. "But I'll see what I can do."

Every hour that went by without news was agony. One minute Kevin was convinced the clerk would never call him back. The next he was certain she'd call him only to torment him with the phone number of a different Rita—some pathetic impostor in Alaska or

New Orleans or Kalamazoo. . . . The hours turned into days, the days into a week.

At last, the clerk called. "Okay, the good news first. I found her number. But . . . " she sighed ominously. "It turned out to be her parents' house. I told them your story and . . ." She let out a little giggle. "Here's her number in Baltimore!"

Two years later, at Kevin and Rita's wedding, Arthur proposed a toast.

"Folks, anytime we find somebody to love, that's a true miracle. But the funny thing is, sometimes God doesn't hand us our miracle on a silver platter. Sometimes He wants us to get out there and work like a dog to make our miracle come true. So, Kevin, you lucky dog. This one's for you!"

—*Peggy Sarlin*

❧

Comment

Some miracles arrive in full bloom and ready for immediate use, while others require careful seeding, a watchful eye, and occasional bouts of superhuman persistence.

I live a hard-scrabble, penny-pinching kind of life. Oh, I'm not complaining; I'm rich in so many other ways—six wonderful children, a great husband, a close-knit family of parents and siblings who are supportive. . . . Yes, there are many blessings in my life for which I'm grateful. Financially, though, we've always had it hard, which is why, at the age of forty-three, I still had not attained my life-long dream of visiting Italy, land of my people, country of my history and heritage. So, when an unexpected little windfall came our way, my husband urged me to take the money and fly (literally and figuratively).

"You've always been last on the list," he said. "Any money we've ever had has always been used for everything and everyone but you. Now it's your turn! Follow your bliss! Fulfill your passion! Seize the moment! *GO!*"

After a lifetime of putting everyone first, I heeded his counsel. I did indeed seize the opportunity. Who could say when it would come again?

I spent eight days in Italy and had the most glorious time. I couldn't do all the touristy things everyone else does: I had made my way there on a tight budget and had to be thrifty with my spending. But I was on a spiritual pilgrimage anyhow, and the holiest of shrines that filled me with such awe and reverence were free. The tourist traps, out of necessity, I avoided.

Still, on my last day, I finally entered a commercial district and ventured into a tourist shop. I had frugally hoarded my dwindling supply of cash reserves so that I could buy mementos of my trip to bring home to my family. After careful selections of gifts for my husband and children were made, I turned my attention to the jewelry showcase, where exquisite necklaces, bracelets, and earrings glittered beckoningly. I found two beautiful necklaces for my mother and sister and motioned the shopkeeper to my side. As he bent to retrieve the two pieces I had selected, my eyes wandered to an exquisite silver-and-turquoise necklace nestled in the corner. I fell in love.

I'm not a materialistic person, and I own very little of value. And I'm not into jewelry, either. But if you're a woman, you know what I mean when I say I fell head over heels, irrevocably in love with that particular piece. Enchanted, captivated, enamored, must-have-it-immediately love. The necklace had my name stamped all over it.

"How much is it?" I asked, tentatively.

The shopkeeper named an outlandish sum. It cost as much as the two necklaces I had chosen for my mother and sister.

Me or them?

I paused for just a moment, deliberating. I really *wanted* that necklace, badly. *Maybe just this once I should put myself first* I thought. Then I said to the shopkeeper in a resolute voice, "Can you gift-wrap the two necklaces in separate boxes, please?"

I returned home, distributed my gifts, and was gratified by both my mother's and sister's delight in my choices. For my own personal keepsake, I had wonderful memories. I never told anyone about the small sacrifice I had made.

Three years later, my mother traveled to Italy, and she, too, returned laden with gifts. My sister and I were in her kitchen, welcoming her home, when she handed us each a box. My sister opened hers first: a breathtaking copper necklace. As I tore the gift wrap off my box, I thought: *Ma always gets us the exact same presents so we won't be jealous; she probably got me the identical copper necklace.* But I was wrong.

For inside the box was the exquisite silver-and-turquoise necklace I had fallen in love with three years before. It was the same exact piece. *How could my mother have known?*

"Ma," I said as calmly and casually as I possibly could. "Did you just hand these boxes to us . . . uhm . . . randomly?"

"Randomly?" my mother asked, puzzled. "What do you mean?"

"I mean . . . did it make any difference to you who got which necklace? When you handed us the boxes, did you *intend* for me to get the silver piece?"

"Oh, but of course!" she exclaimed. "See, I have your name written in small letters on the outside of the box, so I could remember which is which."

"But how come you gave me *this* one?" I persisted. "You usually give us the same exact thing."

"Well, that's true." My mother shrugged her shoulders, seeming just a little perplexed by my question. "I usually *do* give you both the same gift. And I had actually planned to give the two of you the same copper necklaces; the shopkeeper had several of them in the store and I thought they were very attractive . . .

"But then I saw this silver-and-turquoise necklace in the showcase and it caught my eye, so I decided to buy one of each."

"But, Ma," I pressed, "how come you chose it for *me?*"

"Oh, I don't know," she shrugged, dismissively, oblivious to my mounting excitement. "It just somehow reminded me more of you than your sister. I guess you could say it had your name stamped all over it."

Comment

Even simple objects have a mysterious way of reaching their human soulmates.

Vicki Pierson and her husband, John, had always regretted giving up their Irish setter puppy, Randy.

He had been a loyal companion to their six children and a loving presence in their home. Still, when they moved to a new home in Sacramento, California, the landlord said he would allow only one dog. They had another, much older setter by the name of Angel, and he had been with the family a long time. It was wrenching to have to choose between the two, but Vicki reasoned that Angel's chances of being adopted were that much slimmer than Randy's. *A cute puppy has far better prospects than an elderly dog,* she thought.

Heartbroken, but desperately needing to move, the Piersons had no choice but to give Randy up for adoption. When he rode off with his new owner, tears streamed down the children's faces. They were inconsolable. *At least he's in a good home,* Vicki tried to reassure herself.

Time passed but somehow the void left by Randy's absence was never quite filled. The children referred to him constantly, and he was deeply missed. When the Piersons moved again, this time to a larger home where they were able to accommodate a second dog, they decided to search for another Randy.

Vicki called the Irish Setter Rescue League and registered for the first available puppy. Irish setter puppies were hard to come by, she was warned, but Vicki said she would wait.

A few months later, a woman called from the League.

"We know you asked for a puppy," the woman said, "but would you consider adopting an older dog instead?"

She recounted the details of this particular dog's misfortunes—he'd been passed from owner to owner, ending up in the pound—and Vicki was filled with compassion for the dog's sad fate.

"Of course I'll take him!" she said instantly. *Some TLC and the company of six rollicking youngsters will mend him for sure,* she thought.

His name was Ryan, and he seemed completely at ease when they brought him home.

In fact, on his very first night with them, he immediately established himself as a kind of sentinel over the kids. He wandered from room to room, checking on them as they slept.

"Wow!" John Pierson exclaimed. "Randy used to do that, too."

Randy had also liked to rub noses with the family cat, which Ryan proceeded to do as well. As Vicki watched the scene in fascination, she couldn't help but be overcome by the tableau unfolding before her eyes. *Just like Randy,* she thought.

The woman from the Irish Setter League had advised them that Ryan reportedly chewed up furniture and rugs when left alone in a house. A few weeks after they had adopted him, the family went out on a day's outing and had no recourse but to leave Ryan behind. When they returned home, Vicki feared the worst, and braced herself for ruination. But as they opened the door she was relieved to see that everything was in order, exactly as they had left it, and Ryan was contentedly snoozing, curled up the way Randy used to be.

The similarities between Ryan and Randy struck her from time to time, but Vicki thought nothing of it until the day they took Ryan for a walk in a park where Randy used to play. Ryan raced off in search of canine adventures, and, uncharacteristically, didn't heed their command when they called him back. He just kept on racing, and fearful that he would get lost, the Piersons raced right after him—all the way to their *old* home, the first and original home where the first and original Randy used to live!

Now the Piersons really couldn't put their suspicions—or hopes—aside. Vicki thought long and hard about ways she could corroborate the strong hunch she and her husband had about Ryan, and suddenly she remembered that Randy had had a scar on one paw. She called the vet and asked if he would help her determine the truth. He clipped away some fur on Ryan's paw and finally, everything was confirmed. The exact same scar was on Ryan's paw, too. Ryan and Randy were one and the same dog!

"Randy's come back!" the Pierson children squealed in delight.

There had always been that strong bond with Randy—a connection that neither time nor space could diminish. Over the distance of two years and countless neighborhoods, Randy had returned—to his rightful place in the Pierson home.

Comment

What the heart remembers, the mind can never displace.

*W*hen August scorches New York City, nobody wants to cook.

But even the dog days of August were not enough to discourage Ellen and Michael Gibson and their friend Chuck from cooking a gourmet feast.

First the three agreed on an elaborate menu. Then Chuck went to work chopping onions, while Ellen and Michael set out into the Sahara of Manhattan to shop.

An hour later, they returned, lugging bags of groceries and dripping with sweat. As they entered their big, anonymous, modern building, they caught a glimpse of themselves in the lobby mirror.

"Look at us! We're a mess!" said Ellen.

Their hair hung in clumps. Their T-shirts and shorts were soaked with sweat.

In the elevator, Michael pressed the button for the eighteenth floor and said, "First thing, I'm taking a shower."

Carrying their bags, they staggered to their apartment. Ellen kicked open the door. "We're back!"

Thirty people in evening clothes turned and stared at them. Ellen and Michael stared back.

"Who are you?" Michael gasped.

"Who are *you?*" said a perfectly coiffed woman holding a champagne glass.

"We live here," said Michael.

"I'm quite sure *we* do," answered the woman.

"Is this 18C?" Ellen asked.

"17C, I'm afraid. I'm Susie Smith. Won't you come in?"

"Oh, no, we couldn't," said Ellen. "I'm so sorry we bothered you. We're not dressed for a party, as you can . . . "

"Please join us." A smiling man walked towards them and held out his hand. "I'm Rod Smith. Let me get you something cold to drink."

Forgetting all about poor Chuck, who was still faithfully chopping onions in 18C, Ellen and Michael Gibson stepped inside. Within a few minutes, they were chatting with Rod and Susie Smith as if they had known them forever. They were amazed to discover how much they had in common and how greatly they enjoyed each other's company.

That was twelve years ago, and the Gibsons and the Smiths have been best friends ever since. And they still love to laugh about the ridiculous coincidence that brought them together one hot August night.

—*Peggy Sarlin*

Comment

In life, as in cooking, sometimes spontaneity is the best ingredient. Fortunately, both couples accepted the unexpected gift of the moment, and the result was a lifetime banquet of friendship.

*W*herever you go, there you are, says the song. But for Colleen Ryan, the lyrics should have been changed to "Wherever you go, there's Dave Cleary."

New York City is often seen as a huge, impersonal metropolis where hordes of strangers robotically stream past each other, never to meet again. Not to Colleen. To her, New York was a small town in which she kept bumping into Dave Cleary over and over again.

The first time she noticed him was waiting for the crosstown bus. He was hard not to notice, being handsome and six feet two inches tall. But what drew her attention was not his good looks. "There's someone who looks happy," she thought, not knowing that he was stealing sidelong glances at her and thinking, "What an exuberant looking girl!"

Throughout the fall of 1996, Colleen and Dave kept spotting each other around the neighborhood: drinking with friends at a bar, waiting for bagels, eating dinner at the local grill. Gradually, their relationship progressed. When they saw each other on the bus or sidewalk, they no longer pretended they didn't notice. Instead, they nodded quickly, almost imperceptibly at each other, as if to say, "Hey there. I sort of know you." Colleen's friends began teasing her about her "bus boy," while Dave's friends ribbed him about "the cute girl in my neighborhood."

One June morning in 1997, Colleen stepped into her office elevator. It was rush hour, a time when the elevator was always packed. But on this morning, only one person entered: Dave Cleary. As she looked at him in astonishment, the doors closed and, for the first time, they were alone.

"I don't think we've formally met," said Dave. "I'm Dave."

"I'm Colleen," she said.

That was all there was to the incident, but looking back upon it, Colleen now thinks it was God's way of telling them that they should get to know each other.

Two months went by before they met again, this time on the crosstown bus. Dave was with a friend, and the three of them chatted pleasantly. "Who is that?" Dave's friend asked him, as soon as Colleen left. "Why don't you ask her out?"

"But I don't really know her," said Dave. "She's just someone I see around."

"So what?" said his friend.

That did it. Colleen had mentioned where she worked during their conversation on the bus. Dave called her office, asked to speak to a Colleen in a pink suit, and invited her to lunch.

Right from their first date, they discovered how much they had in common. They lived three blocks apart. For the last five years, they had worked in the same building. They both loved golf, went to Mass every Sunday, and were fanatically neat.

"I do have a pretty strange hobby though," Dave confessed. "I play the bagpipes."

Colleen let out a shriek. Her whole family was dedicated to Irish step dancing, and to her, bagpipe music was better than rock and roll.

As their romance blossomed, the time came for Colleen's family to meet Dave. In yet another connection between them, the location for the family gathering was eerily convenient: Dave's apartment was directly across the street from her aunt and uncle, on exactly the same level. At the party, Colleen's ninety-eight-year-old grandmother expressed a yearning for bagpipe music. Dave ducked across the street. An hour later, he returned, dressed in full bagpipe regalia, ready to tirelessly oblige Grandma's every request. Her family happily conceded: Here indeed was Colleen's dream man.

At their wedding in December 1998, Dave played the bagpipes while Colleen step danced jubilantly with her sisters. "I can't believe it," she said. "I'm married to the stranger I met on the bus!"

—*Peggy Sarlin*

Comment

Sometimes miracles only arrive when we're ready to receive them. Dave and Colleen had worked in the same building, riding the same elevator for five years. Yet somehow they had never noticed each other before. Perhaps that was because both of them were involved with other people.

Once those relationships ended, Colleen says, "That's when it started to happen. That's when we started seeing each other everywhere we went. You know, maybe it wouldn't have worked if we'd met five years earlier. We've both done so much, learned so much from other people. All I know is—it sure works now!"

*W*e waited a long time for grandchildren. At a wedding on a Wednesday evening in June, a friend in similar straits (her married son was childless) inquired whether our oldest daughter Shoshana had adoption in mind. Without thinking, I answered, "Yes. A friend of hers in Texas will soon deliver a baby and it will be for her and David."

Even as I glibly uttered those words, I gasped in disbelief. From where had that remark come? As far as I knew, no adoption was in the offing at all. There was no evidence to suggest it. That statement had arrived and left like the wind—without forethought or logic.

But only two days later, on Friday morning, Shoshana called at the crack of dawn from the Midwest, where she lived, to announce that a friend in Texas had just delivered a little boy. She and David were at the airport on their way to Houston to pick him up.

At that point, my two-day-old prediction had vanished from consciousness. In the thrill of the moment, I neglected to inquire, "Where and how can I reach you?" I was totally cut off from our new grandchild, until that night when I awoke just before sunrise. I saw my dead uncle Ben standing at the foot of the bed *demanding* that we name this newborn after him.

Uncle Ben, deceased for about twenty-five years, had never demanded. He was a gentle soul; childless himself, he doted generously and joyfully on his nieces and nephews. But childless, he had left behind neither heir nor namesake. That night, I felt an urgency that frightened me; it seemed almost as though the infant absolutely required the blessings of Uncle Ben and his name in order to flourish.

I was convinced that Shoshana would not acquiesce. She mentioned long ago that her son would be called Noah, and surely she would consider my saga straight out of *Fiddler on the Roof*.

"Let it go," my friends said. I agitated with my husband. "Forget it," he said. Not a soul was on Uncle Ben's side.

The newborn had been six weeks premature and would not be named for another month, when the family would convene for the circumcision. My husband, hoping that I would calm down, asked Shoshana not to divulge the baby's name until that time "for good luck."

Minor surgery was scheduled for me just a few days before the circumcision. My daughter Naomi arrived from out of town to see me and attend the ceremony.

"If anything should happen to me," I said to Naomi, "please tell Shoshana that I had longed for the baby to be named Benjamin."

Naomi gaped at me, her eyes wide.

"Didn't you know?" she said. "He's been Ben since the day he was born."

— *Frieda Englard*

*H*ow embarrassing.

Inching towards the tollbooth at the Verrazano-Narrows Bridge in Staten Island, New York, Morris Benun had just fumbled in his pocket for his wallet when he realized with consternation that it was not there. As the long line of cars slowly snaked their way across the toll plaza, Morris checked the dashboard, the car seats, the floor beneath him. Not there.

How was he going to pay the toll and get home?

Anxiously scanning the cars stretched across the toll plaza in an endless procession, Morris searched for a familiar face.

He was in luck.

Sitting in a car several lanes away was a man with whom Morris was vaguely acquainted: David Mamiye. Morris put his car in park, dashed across the lanes that separated him from David, hastily explained his dilemma, and David reached for his wallet graciously. He extracted the toll and handed it to Morris with a cheerful smile and genuine warmth.

"Pleasure to help you out," he told Morris.

"Hey, thanks. Next time I see you, I'll give it back," said Morris as he sprinted back to his car.

"Forget about it!" shouted David. "Hey, it's only a dollar!"

Twelve years later, Morris was leaving Mount Sinai Hospital in Manhattan, where he had been visiting his wife, who had just given birth. As he approached his car, he noticed with chagrin that he had just preempted an offensive attack by a Department of Transportation officer, who was grimly issuing tickets to cars whose meters had expired. Morris stole a look at the car parked behind his and observed that the time on the meter had expired. Out of the corner of his eye, he watched the officer's determined approach.

What a shame for this person to have to get a fifty-dollar ticket, he thought.

Impulsively, he pulled four quarters out of his pocket and slipped them into the meter, just as the officer advanced toward the car.

At the same time, the unknown owner of the car advanced as well, absorbing with his eye the scene: the officer's rapid approach and Morris's preemptive strike, as the quarters slid quickly into the slot.

"Hey, thanks a lot!" said David Mamiye, whom Morris hadn't seen in twelve years.

They regarded each other in astonishment and awe.

David too was returning from a visit to Mount Sinai, where *his* wife had just given birth.

They smiled at each other in recognition, remembering the dollar at the Verrazano-Narrows Bridge — the dollar that Morris had not yet had the opportunity to repay.

Until now.

"Hey, one good deed deserves another!" exclaimed Morris jovially, as he shook hands with David and drove off.

They were as poor as church mice. Or, perhaps, "synagogue mice" would be the more apt expression, since they were, after all, Jewish. They were "returnees to Judaism" (*baalei teshuva* is the Hebrew idiom of choice) who had renounced the secular, assimilated Jewish backgrounds from whence they hailed and had chosen to adopt a more fervent, religious lifestyle instead.

When they had renounced their roots, their wealthy parents had in turn renounced *them*, cutting them off from their respective families, cutting them out of their inheritances. So, when they decided to get married, the wedding was a simple and spartan affair. No *Goodbye Columbus* opulence for them. No groaning smorgasbord or chopped liver molds carved into elaborate centerpieces. It was stark simplicity all the way.

The wedding had seemed plain and modest enough, but by comparison, the *sheva brochos* celebrations (seven traditional evening feasts that consecutively follow the wedding) were downright austere. On the first night, some herring and crackers were served in a friend's shabby basement apartment. But if the immediate surroundings were, let us say, limited, the joy and happiness that vibrated in the small, modest space was unbridled and abundant. What was lacking in materialistic bounty was more than made up for by the spiritual splendor that radiated throughout the room. When it was time to go home, however, no limousine, town car or even cab awaited their departure as is common practice in the Jewish community. They took the humble subway instead.

They were on the A train, traveling from Washington Heights to their Brooklyn home late at night, riding through some rough neighborhoods. But they weren't wary of their surroundings; they had eyes only for each other—eyes that were filled with shining light.

"My dearest wife," said the smitten husband, "how I wish I could cover you in the finest of jewels and the most beautiful of clothes. . . . How I wish I could take you on a proper honeymoon to some lush resort. . . . At the very least," he cried out in frustration, "if only I could take you now . . . during *sheva brochos* . . . to a sumptuous, lavish, deluxe hotel where the beauty of your soul would be matched by the beauty of your environment. It hurts me so that we have to return now to such a dingy, cramped place! I feel as if I have failed you by not providing you with what almost every groom provides his wife."

"My dear husband," she said gently, "does it not say in the scriptures that where there is love, two people can live together on the edge of a pin? You are all I need."

"You are all I need, too, my sweetest soul mate. Yet how I wish . . ." He bit his lips in vexation.

Just then the doors of the subway train opened, and their intense concentration was broken by the sounds of a song being crooned by a black man in tattered clothing and scraggly beard who had just entered the car. They noticed, in passing, that they were at 125th Street in Harlem.

The man appeared to be in an alcoholic stupor, and they were a little discomfited. It was past midnight, and no one else was in the car but them.

The man made an immediate beeline for the strap overhanging their seat and stared down at them intensely. He began to chuckle.

"Hey, brother and sister!" he shouted. "Are you two *in love?*"

They responded politely, "We just got married last night."

"Whoaa, last night!" he whistled. "That's real heavy. Congratulations, brother and sister!"

"Thank you," they responded courteously. "And how are *you* doing tonight?"

"Oh, I'm just fine, just fine, thank you. Couldn't be better. I feel really good now, seeing two people in love. How'd you meet?"

And so the conversation went, back and forth, all the way to midtown Manhattan. The pair had lost their fear of the man immediately and spoke to him as they would anyone else. They disregarded his alcohol breath. He was, after all, a human being, just like them.

At Forty-second Street, he said good-bye and moved to exit the doors. "Hey, great talking to you!" he said in farewell. "You're nice kids."

As the doors closed behind him, he swirled around suddenly and shouted: "Hey, catch! It's a wedding gift!"

He swiftly hurled a small shopping bag in their direction. Reflexively, the husband opened his arms and caught the bundle, but when he turned to ask the man what he had thrown at them, he was gone. The subway was already in motion, and it was too late to give it back. The pair ran to the windows to see if they could spot the man at a distance, but he had already vanished.

"Let's guess before we open it," the husband proposed playfully. "What do you think is inside?"

"Newspapers?" his wife suggested. "Soda cans? Clothing?"

It was five hundred dollars in cash.

They stared at each other in shock and awe.

"Well," the husband said slowly, "let's get off at the next stop and find one of those gorgeous, magnificent, opulent hotels that I was just talking about."

"I don't understand," his wife said, shaking her head in confusion. "He wore the tattered clothes of a vagrant . . . he seemed homeless . . . he was drunk . . . how did he have five hundred dollars on him and why did he give it to *us*?

"Who *was* that guy?" she asked in wonder.

The husband mulled over her question thoughtfully, as mystified as she, and then finally said:

"Legend has it that Elijah the Prophet disguises himself as a poor wayfarer in order to wander among the common folk and perform good deeds."

"What do we know! What do any of us ever really know?"

"Maybe we just met Elijah the Prophet and we never even recognized him."

— Originally told by Rabbi Shlomo Carlebach,
retold by Yitta Halberstam

❧

Comment

God's messengers are often difficult to recognize, but their message is unmistakably clear.

$\mathcal{I}n$ 1965, the 6th battalion of the Royal Australian Regiment joined American forces involved in combat in the Vietnam War. Many of the young Australian soldiers fought (side by side with American troupes) in the Battle of Long Tan, the biggest and longest day battle the Australians fought in Vietnam.

Each soldier, regardless of his country, received the same standard kit as he set out to fight, including: boots, fatigues, burying head gear and an I.D. tag, otherwise known as a "dog tag," inscribing vital personal details about the soldier. The more fortunate soldiers brought them home from the war and saved them as souvenirs. Sometimes, tragically, the dog tag arrived home from battle without its brave owner.

Thirty years after the war, twenty-nine ex-servicemen from the same Australian regiment decided that they would return to Vietnam to retrace their individual histories during the war. Several of them still harbored disturbing feelings about the horrors they had endured. Dave Newsome viewed his Vietnam year as a twelve-month nightmare. He would have much preferred spending that period of time experiencing his new baby boy's first year in the world.

Dave thought he could possibly free himself of the torment of his memories by returning to the site where his nightmare took place. He and his friend Martin Abbey, along with several other buddies, booked a flight to Vietnam and made their way back to the very spot they had raged in battle thirty years before. They walked around the grounds and recalled the fellow soldiers they had lost and those maimed. They felt profound gratitude for having returned home to their loved ones alive and well.

A young Vietnamese boy glided toward them on his bicycle. He hopped off and walked over to David. Holding out his hand, he revealed a small silver object. David stood before him, baffled, thinking, "Why is this sprite Vietnamese kid singling me out?" He looked into the boy's hand and noticed a beat-up dog tag, resembling the ones that the Vietnam vets wore. "For sale," the boy said in stilted English. Dave flipped the tag over in his hands in order to see the name inscription, wondering which poor soldier left this world without it, or better, left for home without it. Either way, he expected to read an unfamiliar name—just one out of a few million men who had fought in that gruesome war.

Dave raised the tag closer to his face to get a better look at the inscription. He fell back as if a blast of wind hit him and struggled to catch his breath. "I can't believe this! Guys, get a load of this! It says David Newsome!" He read on, recognizing all his personal information.

"Where did you find this?!" he asked the little boy.

"My father," he replied. "He find and give to me. He say people come buy it."

Dave had gone back to a tormented time in his past to retrieve a piece of himself left behind. Now he stood there, embraced by his buddies, holding that piece in the palm of his hand.

*R*upert Hiztig was all of nineteen years old when he ventured to Europe on his first summer break from college with his buddies David and John. The first stop in their adventure was Spain, where they saw the Fiesta de San Fermín, otherwise known as "Running with the Bulls." Afterward they journeyed to France, Germany, and then Denmark.

And that's where Rupert stopped—because he met a lovely Danish girl named Uta. He stayed on in Denmark with her while David and John went on to see the Louvre, in Paris.

As the days wore on and Rupert and Uta enjoyed themselves together, Rupert lost track of time and money. Before he knew it, he realized that his free charter flight back to college in Boston was leaving within two days, and he had a mere $18 left to his name. Rupert hurriedly packed his things, said a tearful good-bye to Uta, and hitchhiked his way through Germany to catch the charter in Paris. When he arrived in Paris, dazed and frazzled from his travels, he was stunned to learn that the plane had left just two hours earlier. Searching his pockets, Rupert discovered that now he had only $8 remaining and no way to get home, to get back to Uta, or to replenish his resources.

There he stood—a teenager, alone, in France, with no money and no ticket home. Rupert felt totally lost and on the verge of tears. Gathering his strength, he began walking through the bustling streets of the Parisian neighborhood. Just as he was about to drop from exhaustion, he noticed a small sign in front of a little inn, promising a bed, a meal, and a bath for just $8—exactly the amount Rupert had left in his pocket. With nowhere else to go and no idea what else to do, Rupert gladly entered the quaint little establishment.

An elderly woman sat stooped over a desk.

"I need . . . a . . . room," said Rupert slowly, clearly, and loudly, hoping the woman would understand his English.

"Monsieur," she replied calmly, and pointed to the ledger, motioning for him to sign his name. Rupert wrote in clear, legible letters: RUPERT HITZIG, and turned the ledger back to the woman.

She looked at the name, cocked her head to the side, and said in a heavy French accent, "Hitzig? Another Monsieur Hitzig is here."

"What?" exclaimed Rupert. "Can't be." *After all*, he thought to himself, *how many Hitzigs are there? It's such an unusual name. And what would he be doing here?*

"What is the other Mr. Hitzig's first name?" Rupert inquired.

"Peter," she responded.

"*Peter?*" shouted Rupert. "That's my brother!"

Rupert had no idea that Peter was even in Europe, and now, his older brother was here, in this very same inn! At first Rupert stood flabbergasted, his mind racing through the course of events that led to this remarkable moment. His next thought was . . . *money! . . . I'll bet he'll have money*.

"What room is Peter in?" asked Rupert, flooded with a mix of emotions.

"Room 420," the woman replied, smiling at this excitable boy standing before her.

Within moments, Rupert pounded with unleashed fervor on the door of room 420, unable to contain his anticipation for his brother's shocked expression and their joyful reunion. After what seemed like a millennium, Peter opened the door, stared expressionless at the frantically wide-eyed familiar face and grunted these older-brother precious pearls of love, "What do YOU want?"

*E*very religion has its holy shrines, its sacred spaces, its hallowed sites. These are places that pilgrims believe are filled with the Divine presence, where the very atmosphere throbs with spiritual energy, and where petitions and prayers are thought to be particularly blessed.

In Judaism, the most famous of these is the Western Wall, located in Jerusalem. But in Israel—in the Galilee, near the ancient city of Safed—there is another, lesser-known spot to which some make their way, and the remote terrain in which it is located is wild and untamed. Yet despite the rough trip, thousands travel there faithfully each year in hope of a special miracle. The miracle of love.

For Amuka, as the mystical burial site of Rabbi Yonatan Ben Uziel is called, is legendary as the sanctuary to which unmarried men and women retreat as a last resort. It is believed that Amuka particularly graces the supplications of singles, who immerse themselves in prayer at the grave of the holy sage. Before his death, Rabbi Ben Uziel told his disciples that when he arrived in Heaven, he would dedicate himself to the mission of expediting matches between lonely singles. This legend has made Amuka a popular stopping place for men and women seeking marriage partners.

And so they come, despair written in their eyes, but a still-fluttering last hope deep in their hearts.

Rachel Strauss* was forty-five. Some of her former high school classmates were already expecting their first grandchild, but she had never married. People chided her for being "too picky," and the tactless, rude remarks stung. She was looking for a soul mate, a kindred spirit, the "right one." And, despite her age, she refused to compromise.

Her mother warned her that she wasn't trying hard enough. One day Rachel snapped: "Not trying hard enough! Okay, I'll make that tough trip to Amuka in Israel and pray my heart out. Is that trying hard enough for you?" For many, and for Rachel herself, it was the measure of last resort.

She was embarrassed by her own desperation; she couldn't believe she was going to join the legions of forlorn souls who converged there. Inside, she felt skeptical.

At Amuka, she was directed to the women's side (at Jewish holy sites, men and women pray in separate areas) and handed a prayer book. Despite herself, and in spite of her own inner reservations, emotion surged through her as she prayed. Tears welled up in her eyes and she prayed as she had never prayed before. It seemed as though she had been standing and praying for an eternity when, suddenly, something stirred her from her reverie and made her look up.

Across a long stretch, from the other side of the praying area, a young man was regarding her with intense interest. Despite her usual shyness and reserve, she felt compelled, forced beyond her will, to return his gaze. Their eyes locked.

Rachel felt electric shock waves charge through her body, her very being. She couldn't drop her gaze from the young man's. They stared at each other for a long time. Finally, she shook herself free of the hypnotic state into which she had entered and lowered her eyes in modesty. She continued her prayers. When she finished, she raised her eyes once more and searched for the young man. He was gone.

Her shoulders slumped in disappointment. She had been hoping against hope that the mysterious force that had engulfed her had had significance for him as well. In her wild fantasy, she had hoped that she would find him waiting for her near the women's section, and that he would say to her: *Is it you then? The one I've been praying for all my life?*

But he wasn't there waiting, and she chastised herself for having read too many romantic novels. *I guess it was my imagination*, she concluded sadly. *Or my*

desperation. Thinking Amuka works its magic right
away . . . how pathetic could I get!

Three weeks later, when Rachel was back in the
United States, a matchmaker called her mother and
talked up a terrific young man whom, she maintained, it
would be very worthwhile for Rachel to meet.

"Mother," Rachel said, "I'm sorry, I know it breaks
your heart that I'm single and lonely, but I just can't go
on another blind date again. I just can't."

"Please, Rachel," her mother begged. "Just this last
one. Mrs. Schick* doesn't stop singing his praises; please
try this last time for me—okay, sweetheart?"

Rachel sighed. She knew what anguish her solitary
state caused her mother.

"Last blind date?" she asked her mother.

"Last blind date," her mother promised.

And indeed, it was.

For there, standing on the threshold when she flung
open the door to welcome her blind date, was none other
than the young man from Amuka, the one whose eyes
had locked with hers, the one who had made her shiver
with recognition.

Once again they stared at each other in shock and
acknowledgment, and finally, breaking the silence, he
smiled and said: "I think we've already met."

What he really wanted to say, he told her much
later, were the words he was forced to hold back

because they were not appropriate for a man of his religious background. They would have sounded too bold, too flirtatious, he confessed later after they were married.

But what he really wanted to say when she opened the door, he told her, were the very words that had echoed through her being at Amuka:

Is it you then? The one I've been praying for all my life?

❧

Comment

A lifetime of waiting seems a small price for a love that is truly eternal.

He called them "little angels" and urged us to treat them with sympathy and respect. But long before I had taken my first class on compassion with my spiritual master, I already felt a special affinity with the panhandlers lining the street corners of the most affluent sections of New York, imploring swiftly darting passersby with round and troubled eyes, "Can you spare a little change?"

"Human tollbooths," one media cynic had dismissively described them, outraged by their growing numbers and angered at being imposed upon, his privacy violated, time and time again.

But I felt differently. When an acquaintance—upright, respectable, professional, and wealthy—had a sudden nervous breakdown, disappeared from home, and was found by detectives a week later living on the underground railroad tracks of Grand Central Terminal, my perspective on life was changed irrevocably.

"If it happened to him, it can happen to anyone," a voice whispered within my soul. "Are you so arrogant as to think that you can remain untouched by life's vicissitudes?"

"There but for the grace of God go I" became the motto by which I lived, and from that point forward I began to look at troubled souls differently, with a softer, gentler eye.

So, as my spiritual master instructed, I never gave these panhandlers less than a dollar. Working as I did in

Greenwich Village, which seems to be densely populated by them (perhaps by virtue of the fact that this neighborhood's residents are known to be liberal and particularly tolerant of all kinds of people), I had frequent encounters with these tragic souls.

It was not unusual for several dollars a day to migrate from my pocketbook into their outstretched hands. When it began to seem too much, I would reproach myself: *Would you hesitate for a moment in buying yourself a vegetable juice (three-fifty), a pizza and soda (two and a quarter), a couple of magazines to read over the weekend (ten dollars)? Isn't it more important that this man eat a decent meal?*

And then, to prod myself into feeling more compassionate, I would utter under my breath my favorite mantra: *"There but for the grace of God go I."*

One evening, I was standing outside my office building on Twelfth Street and Broadway, waiting for my husband to pick me up by car. He was, in keeping with timeworn tradition, late. Evening shadows began to draw close, and bizarre-looking creatures (costumed in spiked, studded black leather, purple hair, triple nose rings, and an abundance of tattoos) whom I ordinarily didn't see during the day began to fill the streets. I began to determinedly dwell on my husband's positive attributes and multiple merits in order to distract myself from the knowledge that his customary lateness had placed me in many an unwanted situation.

"Please, ma'am, can you spare some change?" The voice, soft and entreating, broke into my reverie.

A panhandler stood before me in tattered clothes, his manner mild, apologetic. His eyes were gentle and kind and sweet. Despite the harshness of his life, his face was luminous and radiant. There was a certain aura he emanated that made me feel safe. I knew instantly what my spiritual master meant with his incongruous appellation "little angels." Surely this man belonged to that class.

I dug into my pocketbook and began to pull out a dollar bill. It was nestled close to a five. I began to feel the tension of a conflict tug at my temples.

Hey, a dollar is nice enough! one voice within me urged. *How many people even give that much? Don't be a fool; give the dollar, it's more than enough.*

Hey, another inner voice reprimanded, *you're going out to eat with your husband at a fancy restaurant. The tab will probably amount to at least fifty dollars. Doesn't this poor broken man deserve to eat too?*

I gave him the five.

His mouth crinkled into a large grin, and his eyes lit up.

"Oh thank you, ma'am!" he said effusively. "You don't know how much this means to me. I haven't eaten a decent meal for days."

I nodded my head in acknowledgment and he began to walk away. A minute later, he made a U-turn and wheeled back to my side.

"I want to thank you again and shake your hand," he announced magnanimously, extending his arm in an almost chivalrous way. I looked at his grimy hand dubiously. It had clearly been unwashed for several days, and it was clearly a hand that rifled through trash bins and garbage. I thought of the bacteria, the germs, the poisons that could seep from his hand to mine.

I also thought of the humiliation he would suffer if I refused his attempt at grace, at regaining the humanity he had surrendered long ago. My head shouted "Refuse!" but my heart would not listen.

Tentatively, I stretched out my hand, and he clasped it with a firm, hearty handshake. He smiled once more and left.

And then he came back again.

"What's your name?" he asked softly.

I was taken aback. All these years that I had distributed money to the panhandlers of New York, most had offered their thanks, some had tipped their threadbare hats, one or two had even said "You're a nice lady," but none had ever asked for my name.

I trusted this man, but for some strange reason that I still can't fathom, I lied and told him that my name was Alexandra. I don't lie easily, and I still wonder what made me do it, but lie I did, as I said, "Alexandra. My name is Alexandra."

"Alexandra," he mused. "I'll never forget you, Alexandra. And you know, I'm sure we'll meet again one day."

I smiled at the man's earnest but naive attempt to forge a connection. "Oh, I'm sure we will," I said insincerely.

"Well, good-bye again," he said halfheartedly, seemingly reluctant to leave.

My husband's car pulled up at the curb.

"What's *your* name?" I asked almost as an afterthought as I glanced at the car in relief.

"James," he answered.

"Well, good-bye, James, and good luck to you."

"See you soon," he smiled.

Yeah, sure, I thought.

All night long, I was pensive. I thought of the interchange that had taken place between James and myself, and how hard he had tried to give something back. There were people in my own life who were *not* panhandlers who could learn a thing or two about reciprocity from James, I thought. And I fancied that, just as my spiritual master had sometimes implied, there was something almost holy about a panhandler like James.

Two years later, deeply engrossed in my thoughts, I stepped off a curb at a busy intersection at Broadway and Forty-second Street. A horn blared and a woman screamed. I had stepped right into the path of an oncoming car.

"Alexandra, look out!" a voice shouted in warning, but my mind didn't register the significance of that name.

Suddenly, I felt a strong hand pull me away and back up to the curb. The car whizzed by, just inches from where I had stood a second ago. I turned around to face my benefactor.

It was James.

I gazed at him in disbelief, thunderstruck. He, however, didn't seem to share my surprise at all.

"I told you we would meet again," he smiled sweetly.

He stretched out his hand once again—the hand into which I had tentatively dropped the five-dollar bill; the hand that I had shaken with such unease.

The firm, strong hand that had saved my life.

We shook hands once again and then James disappeared into the crowd.

"Little angels," my spiritual master had called them. How had he known?

Kelly McAdam

❦

Comment
Spiritual teachers come in many strange disguises.

*W*hen Karen found out that another baby was on the way, she did what she could to help her three-year-old son Michael prepare for the new sibling. Karen knew she was having a girl, and she spoke to her son often about the upcoming birth. Michael awaited it with eager anticipation. Day after day and night after night, Michael sang to his sister in Mommy's tummy. He was building a bond of love with his little sister before he even met her.

The pregnancy progressed normally for Karen. In time, the labor pains came. Soon they were coming every five minutes. Then every three, every two, and finally every minute. Karen was rushed to the delivery room, and there some serious complications set in. Karen was told that a C-section might very well be required. Finally, Michael's little sister was born.

There was intense joy and reverence at the moment of birth, but the joy quickly gave way to grave concern. The little baby was in serious condition. With a siren howling in the night, the ambulance rushed the infant to the neonatal intensive care unit at St. Mary's Hospital in Knoxville, Tennessee. The pediatric medical team there began working immediately on the baby, but it seemed she would need an enormous amount of care over the next few weeks if she were to stand a fighting chance.

The days inched by with the newborn quite a distance from home. To make matters worse, the little girl's condition seemed to be getting graver as time wore on. "There is very little hope," said the pediatric specialist. "Be prepared for the worst." With deep pain and sorrow, Karen and her husband contacted a local cemetery about a burial plot. They had fixed up a special room in their home for the new baby, but now it seemed as though they were going to plan for a funeral instead.

Michael, however, kept begging his parents to let him see his sister. "I want to sing to her," he kept saying. As week two in intensive care began, it looked as if a funeral would come before the week was over. Michael kept nagging about singing to his sister, but kids are never allowed in intensive care. Karen made up her mind, though. She would take Michael in whether they liked it or not! If he didn't see his sister then, he might never have a chance to see her alive.

She dressed him in an oversized scrub suit and marched him into the ICU. He looked like a walking laundry basket. But the head nurse recognized him as a child and bellowed, "Get that kid out of here now! No children are allowed!" Maternal rage rose up strong in Karen, and the usually mild-mannered woman glared steely-eyed right into the head nurse's face, her lips a firm line. "He is not leaving until he sings to his sister!"

Karen towed Michael to his sister's bedside. He gazed at the tiny infant losing her battle to live. After a moment, he began to sing. In the pure-hearted voice of a three-year-old, Michael sang: "You are my sunshine, my only

sunshine, you make me happy when skies are gray."
Instantly the baby girl seemed to respond. Her pulse rate
began to calm down and became steady. "Keep on singing,
Michael," encouraged Karen with tears in her eyes.

"You'll never know, dear, how much I love you, please
don't take my sunshine away." As Michael sang to his
sister, the baby's ragged, strained breathing became as
smooth as a kitten's purr.

"Keep on singing, sweetheart!" Karen encouraged.

"The other night, dear, as I lay sleeping, I dreamed I
held you in my arms . . .," he sang.

Michael's little sister began to relax, as rest, healing
rest, seemed to sweep over her.

"Keep on singing, Michael." Tears had now conquered
the face of the bossy head nurse. Karen glowed.

"You are my sunshine, my only sunshine. Please don't
take my sunshine away . . .," the little boy's voice rang out.

The next day . . . the very next day . . . the little girl was
well enough to go home! *Woman's Day* magazine called it
"The Miracle of a Brother's Song." The medical staff just
called it a miracle. Karen called it a miracle of God's love.

◦◦◦

Comment
When love sings its purest song, the gates of Heaven
fling open.

*T*hey loved each other fiercely, but battled furiously, and often. They were young, passionate, impetuous, and their arguments were intense and untamed. The sad truth was that the Colligans* — everyone's favorite couple, the unknowing public's oft-pointed-to prime example of the "perfect match" — just couldn't get along.

The tumultousness of their marriage was captured and crystallized by Tim Colligan's frequent stab at dark humor. "I love you madly," Tim often told his wife Betsy when he was particularly vexed, "but I sure do hate your guts!"

After several years of deadlocks, standoffs and stalemates, they finally decided to call it quits. Too many accusations, recriminations and provocations had turned the marriage sour. "I can't live without you, but I can't live with you, either," Tim grimaced, still unflaggingly wry.

The Colligans divorced, and drifted away from one another. Soon they were oceans apart — literally. Tim moved to America, while Betsy remained behind in England. They lost track of their respective spouses' whereabouts, and went on to rebuild new lives. But Tim was never able to put Betsy out of his mind completely.

He had fallen into the habit of comparing the current women in his life to his fond memories of Betsy, whose virtues had become embellished over time. He found these women lacking in her tempestuous temperament which had excited his blood, and her passion for life which had spurred his own. His dates were too docile, compliant and passive. Didn't any woman possess the fiery nature of his first wife?

But then he remembered the inflammatory statements and the stinging remarks that had punctuated his previous marriage, and he shook himself out of the yearning into which he was prone to lapse.

"Have you forgotten what a nightmare those years were?" he chided himself. "A nightmare from hell."

Years passed and Tim remained single and alone. Not for lack of trying, though. He truly wanted to get married, and he vigorously pursued every lead, every scent of trial, every signpost pointing to the perfect woman. But all leads eventually ran cold.

Tim tried singles parties, singles weekends, even matchmaking services. He was besieged with names and numbers of eligible women, overwhelmed by the zeal of well-meaning friends. But no woman ever came close to his ideal—now fully mythologized—named Betsy.

Two decades later, Tim was now older and wiser but still solitarily single. With the passage of time, however, a new window of opportunity had opened. It was called the computer, and matchmaking services on the new technology had come into vogue and were all the rage. "Well, why don't you try a computer dating service then?" Tim's friends sensibly suggested, pointing out that he had exhausted every other possibility.

Tim, weary after all these years, but still fervent about finding the "right one," agreed to try the newest craze. He was referred to a quality computer dating service and filled out many forms that asked detailed questions about his life, likes and dislikes, personality traits, and so on. His answers would be run through the computer and he would be matched up with the prospects deemed most appropriate for him. He would receive one name and number at a time, the people who manned the service told him, with the candidate the computer regarded as the strongest heading the top of the list.

Tim answered all the questions on the forms in a rigorously honest way ("no use fooling a computer" he shrugged) and waited with eager anticipation for the name of the first—and most viable—prospect to arrive in the mail.

When he tore open the envelope from the computer dating service, Tim stared in shock at the name the computer had designated as the most desirable candidate of all.

Sifting, sorting and culling from hundreds of thousands of names worldwide, the computer had selected none other than BETSY COLLIGAN of London—his very own ex-wife—as the perfect match for Tim!

After regaining his wits, Tim chuckled, his wry humor still intact.

"Hmmm," he said, a broad grin plastered all over his face, "maybe the computer knows something that I don't know?"

So, he picked up the phone, and dialed an international number to a woman from whom he needed no formal introduction.

And they've been happily remarried ever since.

I have witnessed a story of how two people were linked that could never be relegated to chance. It is about my own brother and his doctor.

The story goes back to when I was eleven years old and we lived in Albany, New York. At the time, my parents rented the top floor of one of those typical three-story city houses, joined by common walls on both sides and forming rows of brick buildings, like cutouts or clones, on both sides of the long streets. There was one "flat," as the apartments were then called, under us and another in the basement.

The owners, Mr. and Mrs. Lizzi, lived in the basement. They were a lovely older Italian couple with a few grown children. One of their sons had recently married a beautiful young woman newly arrived from Italy, and he and his wife lived in the middle flat. My job that summer was to take care of my little brother Joey, then three years old. He mostly loved to ride his tricycle up and down the sidewalk, and many times I was fiercely bored. One thing that helped a lot was being able to spend some time with my young neighbor on the second floor, now a happy mother-to-be.

They called her "Catuzza," which meant, my father told me, "sweet little Catherine." The "-uzza" was a diminutive that Italians put at the end of a name when a child was particularly sweet, and it usually stuck until adulthood. Catuzza was indeed sweet, and I loved to be near her.

By summer, Catuzza was well into her pregnancy and lonely since her husband, a shoemaker, worked long hours to provide for his budding family. She knew very little English, so I would help her learn and Joey would put in his two cents' worth. He had golden curls, and she would twine these around her fingers. Her smile would always make me feel that she was wondering about her own child in her womb.

Sometimes when the baby would kick, she would let me touch her stomach, and once, when Joey was close by, he too put his hand on her stomach, feeling the baby kick. I told him that was her baby moving inside her, and Joey kind of glowed with fascination. Catuzza was embarrassed. In those days children weren't supposed to know about babies being in a mother's tummy.

At summer's end, we moved, and I lost track of Catuzza. My brother Joey Oppedisano grew up to join the U.S. Army, go to college, establish a career with the New York State Labor Department—and to contract a fatal illness at age thirty-five.

I shall never forget the day. I was restless at the university where I was working on Long Island in late 1972. I kept thinking of my family in Albany all day, and finally at 4 P.M. I picked up the phone and called my sister Rosemary. "How did you know?" she asked me. "How did I know what?" I answered.

She told me—that day my brother Joe had been in surgery since early morning as the doctors removed a swollen spleen. Considering the degree of malignancy, they didn't want to take bets on how long he would live. Sometime after that, when I visited Joe, he told me that he had had this strange experience. He "saw" the inside of his body and all through him were little bristles, like those on a brush.

This didn't make much sense until the lab reports were all back and Joe's doctor gave him the news. He had a fatal disease called hairy cell leukemia, and the doctor, to explain to him what this meant, showed him what Joe had already "seen" in his strange and unexplainable visualization—"hairy" cells under the microscope.

Now the battle began, and Joe, with the family's intense support, was determined to live. There was one strong ray of hope—in the doctor he eventually found, a hematologist named Dr. Frank Lizzi, well respected at St. Peter's Hospital in Albany.

This was a familiar name to me, and one day when I was visiting Joe in the hospital, I told him that when he was a tot, we had lived in a house on Irving Street where our landlord was named Lizzi. Joe was aware of that. In fact, he said, our one-time landlord was the late grandfather of his Dr. Lizzi. It was as though a light had gone on. Was Dr. Lizzi's father a shoemaker and his mother named Catuzza? I asked. Yes, said Joe. They

Small Miracles of Love & Friendship   169

were Dr. Lizzi's parents. When he told me that his doctor was only three years younger than himself, I gasped. It hit me how remarkable it was—that Catuzza's baby, yet unborn, was to be the doctor who would save Joe's life.

At that moment, Dr. Lizzi came in. When he put his hands on Joe, what I saw then was not two men, doctor and patient. I saw a golden-haired child with his hand on the tummy of a blushing mother-to-be, and I marveled at the mystery of connections.

Never would anyone have been able to imagine that the unborn child would one day himself return that touch, bringing the miracle of life with it.

Who put the pieces in place that would forever link the lives of these two men? That's the question that rattles the mind of a truth seeker.

—Antoinette Bosco

*M*ary Higgins* was blessed with one child, and he was born profoundly retarded. Although he could not coo contentedly, gurgle happily, or smile up at her in warm recognition as other babies are wont to do, she loved him as wholeheartedly as any mother loves a child. She refused to surrender him to life in an institution, even though that was the very recourse everyone — doctors, social workers, relatives and friends — urged upon her. "Not *my* child!" she swore fiercely. Mary Higgins was of stubborn Irish stock, and there was no contradicting or stopping her. Once Mary made up her mind, her determination was cast in stone. She was, in a word, implacable.

So, despite the entreaties of everyone around her, Mary kept the child and tended him as best as she could. But even her best wasn't good enough. She was not trained in speech therapy, physical therapy, occupational therapy — all therapies that could, at least in small ways, enhance her son's life. When he was a young man, she finally recognized the futility of her efforts and realized that indeed, he needed more than just what love could provide. She sought out the best of institutional care near her home, and, with a heavy heart, transferred him to a facility that was state-of-the-art.

But Mary never abandoned her son. She visited him daily, spending hours with him, bringing with her home-made cookies and little treats, kissing and hugging him as passionately as before. Her devotion never wavered, and she remained a constant presence in his never-changing life.

The son grew older, as did his mother. Her husband died; her friends passed away; her relatives retired to different states. Soon, the only ones Mary had left in the world were her son and a young niece, Christie. It was when her world had shrunk to such small parameters that Mary learned she had liver cancer.

Her niece had accompanied Mary to the doctor's, where the grim diagnosis was handed down. Mary's first words, after she bent her head and covered her face to conceal the tears, were: "Whatever will happen to my son?"

Though the devastating illness ravaged her body, it could never claim her spirit. Mary lingered on—long past the doctors' prognostications—in tremendous pain and suffering. But she wouldn't let go—indeed, she *couldn't* let go because she was worried sick about her son. Who would take care of him after she was dead?

The niece was heartbroken to see her aunt in such agony. "What's the use of her living this way, when it's a living death?" she cried out to the doctors. They looked at her with pity and compassion and answered: "She has a tremendous will to live. *You* know that. And you know *why*."

As the niece witnessed her aunt's tribulations, it was all she could do to restrain herself from pulling out all the tubes and catheters and IV drips to which she was attached and end her misery. "Die already!" she felt like shouting. But of course, she said nothing at all.

One day, the phone call came from the state-of-the-art institution.

It was a genuine mystery, the administrator said, half-apologetically, half-defensively. No one could explain it. He hadn't been ill or anything. He was in excellent health. He hadn't complained the night before or said anything was bothering him. But this morning he had been found lifeless in his bed.

Mary's son was dead.

Mary was told, as gently as possible. Her eyes fluttered open wide and she said enigmatically, "So, it's over then . . . it's been consummated."

A few hours later, she died peacefully in her sleep, a mother in life—and in death.

*H*aving just returned to work from a dental appointment, Jennifer, a buyer for a department store, sat at her desk thinking how much she hated blind dates. She had obliged well-meaning friends by going out on two such dates in the past month, and both had proved disastrous. Now, on a Friday afternoon, she unhappily faced the prospect of spending another evening with a man she knew absolutely nothing about.

As the Novocain wore off and her gum began to throb, Jennifer's mood went from bad to worse. Her dentist had fitted her with a temporary cap to wear on a front tooth that was in the process of being crowned, and she despised the way it looked. Impulsively she picked up the phone to cancel her date. After leaving a message on his answering machine saying that she was sick and couldn't go out, Jennifer felt much better. She was back in control of her life.

Soon after that, her phone rang. It was a girlfriend, Phyllis, calling to invite her to a huge singles party at a downtown hotel. Jennifer jumped at the chance. Now, she figured, she could start choosing her dates herself.

At the party, Jennifer and Phyllis were standing by the buffet, flirting with a group of guys, when Jennifer suddenly sneezed. She sneezed so hard the unthinkable happened. The temporary cap flew off her tooth.

Jennifer watched helplessly as it shot under a nearby food-laden table. Though no one else saw the tooth fly, Jennifer was thoroughly embarrassed. Holding her hand over her mouth, she quickly excused herself, then made a mad dash for the other side of the table. As nonchalantly as possible, she dropped to her hands and knees, lifted the tablecloth and crawled under. After much frantic searching, she finally located the wayward crown.

Crawling toward it, Jennifer suddenly recoiled in horror as a male hand came from nowhere and grabbed the tooth. She looked up to find herself face to face with a waiter who had crawled in from the other side.

"Looking for this?" he laughed, dangling the temporary crown. Jennifer grimaced. "It's okay," he grinned. "I'm only masquerading as a waiter. Working my way through dental school. By the way, my name's Michael."

He handed over her tooth, holding her hand an extra second in the exchange. After slipping the crown back on, Jennifer smiled and relaxed enough to realize that this waiter/dental student was not only charming but good-looking too. When Michael mentioned that he was supposed to be out on a blind date with some "babe" who had canceled on him, Jennifer laughed. She shyly replied that she too was supposed to have gone on a blind date but had figured the guy was a complete nerd so she had canceled also.

"Wait a minute," Michael demanded. "Your name isn't Jennifer Maloney, is it?" One look at her face and Michael knew. "So you're the babe and I'm the nerd!"

They both collapsed in fits of giggles until interrupted by Phyllis, who peered under the table, demanding to know just what was going on.

Michael and Jennifer eventually married, and they recently celebrated their tenth wedding anniversary!

—Jan Wolterman

❧

Comment
When the Universe wishes to bestow a gift, it leaves no table unturned.

*B*eth Donnelly, a practical nurse and Doreen Krakat, a nurse technician, both worked at Van Rensselaer Manor. The two instantly gravitated toward each other, sharing a fondness for wisecracks. Their humorous exchanges served to bond Beth and Doreen as they developed a close friendship over their years at the nursing home.

In October of 1998, Theresa Murphy, Doreen's grandmother joined the patients at the home. Her family thought it would be best for their seventy-seven-year-old loved one to live under medical supervision, considering her emphysema and congestive heart problems. Doreen told Beth that her grandmother had just been admitted to Van Rensselaer, and the two friends dashed to Mrs. Murphy's room to give her a warm welcome.

On the bureau, Doreen noticed her grandmother's family album and slowly leafed through it.

"Can I look with you?" Beth inquired.

Without hesitation, Doreen went through the photos with her chum. Beth's eyes fixed on a photograph of an infant. She felt her heart quicken and her mouth go dry.

"Who's that?" she asked, her voice quivering.

"That's Hope Ann, the baby my mother gave up for adoption."

Beth's blood abruptly rose to her face and she practically choked on her next words.

"That baby is me," she swallowed hard. "I was Hope Ann!"

Doreen forced a grin, thinking this was another one of Beth's gags. Realizing Beth was dead serious, she agreed to look into the matter. At first, she felt reluctant to bring up the topic with her mother. After all, it must have been a terribly painful decision for her to give up her child forever. When Doreen summoned up the courage to ask her mom, she soon discovered that, indeed, she and Beth—her closest friend at work—shared the same mother.

Twenty-seven years prior, Doreen's mother, Theresa Okonsi, gave birth to a baby girl she named Hope Ann. Overwhelmed by the prospect of becoming a mother and caring for an infant, she sought counseling. A social worker suggested that she consider giving her baby up for adoption. Feeling she had no other recourse, she gave up her baby. Hope Ann joined a loving family named Donnelly, who named her Beth and chose an open and honest policy regarding her adoption.

Although Beth viewed the Donnellys' with all her heart and mind as her parents, she often wondered about her birth mother and couldn't help but question whether she thought of her as well. And, in fact, she did. Theresa Okonski resisted the desire to search for Beth, assuming her daughter wouldn't want her to. So they both suppressed the longing to reunite deep inside their hearts.

Through the course of distinct life events, each one serving as a stepping stone to the next, a long-withheld heart's wish came at last to fruition.

*B*renda Tucker was no stranger to challenge. As the single mother of two girls, Brenda was hard-working and self-sacrificing. She knew early on in motherhood that her children came first.

Brenda was a veteran caretaker. She had tended to her sick mother during her childhood while also caring for her five brothers and sisters. Brenda found it hard to take time just for herself. Moving from a dependent family to an abusive husband and ultimately to single motherhood, Brenda found little reason to give herself the gifts most people take for granted—long walks, outings with friends, freedom even to just do nothing. She suffered from self-inflicted guilt and believed that she was undeserving of the finer things. She chose to pass on freedom and resign herself to work, sleep, and caring for her girls. At this point in Brenda's life, it was all she could commit to.

In the summer of 1981, Brenda was working as a secretary in Houston, Texas. Time was a commodity and money was for survival. A company softball team was forming, and Brenda elected to join. It was the first time in her entire life that she had made a decision with just fun in mind. No consequence, no pain, no pressure, just fun. Brenda was very excited. She looked forward to making new friends, getting some fresh air and exercise, and enjoying the sun.

Her mood was great until she got the bulletin. All players needed tennis shoes—a detail she had neglected to consider. Of course softball players would need tennis shoes, but Brenda, a novice, hadn't considered that before she signed up on the company roster. Now what was she to do? It was only weeks earlier that she had had to decide which light bulb was most in need of replacement because she could ill afford the luxury of light in every room. She couldn't possibly buy new shoes, but could she swallow her pride and back out of the league? She could not. She would not.

Brenda had begun to hit bottom. Depressed, anxious, and most of all prideful, she knew she had to cancel the one event in her life that would bring her peace and joy. And she knew that no one could know why. Taking handouts and accepting pity were not what Brenda was made of. She would think up an excuse and back out gracefully. In the meantime, she needed to attend to the struggle of the day-to-day. She drove to the grocery store still troubled and still wondering what to say to her coworkers the next day. As she ran through plausible excuses in her mind, she parked her car and got out. But in that moment, Brenda happened on what was an unmistakable gift next to her car door.

A shoe box.

"Someone must have left these here," thought Brenda and decided to enter the store without them to give the owner a chance to retrieve the shoes.

Over an hour passed, and when she returned to her car, groceries in hand, the shoebox lay untouched. The second thought crossed Brenda's mind. "They couldn't be my size." Brenda had a below-average shoe size of 5½—difficult to find in shoe stores, much less in parking lots. The curiosity finally got to her and she opened the box. Inside was a brand-new pair of Nikes sized to fit a 5½ foot. Brenda couldn't believe her eyes. After much deliberation, she finally decided to take the shoes home, and, unsurprisingly, they were a perfect fit.

Unbeknownst to Brenda, the gift, disguised as a simple pair of shoes, was actually a key that unlocked and freed a side of Brenda she had never met before and before long had come to love.

※

Comment
Since self love is God's love, the most important act of friendship is towards oneself.

It was hot as we were driving the back roads of the Texas hill country in the middle of August. I looked over at my husband, J.W., feeling so grateful to have him at my side. The past year had left us all feeling battered and vulnerable. I thought of my mom, waving from her porch as we drove away that morning, her eyes full of a year's worth of sorrow and pain that had culminated the day before in the heartwarming memorial service held for my brother, Skeeter. He was only forty-seven years old. We had all clung together during the past year, sharing our strength and letting our love for Skeeter flow over him. But now, we were exhausted and drained, and ready to go home.

On our way to Los Angeles, J.W. and I had decided to spend our last night with my younger brother, Sonny, and my sister-in-law, Lisa. Skeeter and Sonny had always been as close as two brothers could possibly be and I knew that Sonny was reeling. Being the big sister, I wanted to make sure he was going to be okay before I flew fifteen hundred miles away. Besides, I hoped that sharing memories could somehow ease our pain and loss.

Like my mom, Sonny lived just outside a tiny Texas town, and as we drove down the long driveway leading to his house, the countryside held healing powers of its own, bringing to me a measure of peace and calm.

I closed my eyes and Skeeter's face loomed before me. It was no longer filled with the consuming pain of the terrible cancer, no longer swollen and discolored from the myriad medicines he was given. His smile was real. I knew in my heart that he was in a happier place, but I regretted our unfinished business.

As brother and sister will, we had secretly plotted one day as I sat beside his bed. That day had been a good one—the pain at bay—and we were talking about what heaven would be like. Even though I knew Skeeter would be safe and happy there, I suggested that it would be a great idea for us to work out some sort of signal between us—something that would let me know that he had made the journey and that heaven was all we expected it to be. He thought it was a great idea, and we agreed to come up with an appropriate signal. Unfortunately, time to think was not a luxury we could afford, and then it slipped away. So now I had to be satisfied with my own belief that Skeeter was smiling down on us from heaven. My confirmation would have to come from my prayers, and that was enough.

I felt the car stop, and my reverie was interrupted by Sonny's big hello and warm hugs all around. Later that evening, as we sat on the back deck with Sonny and Lisa, the Texas sky was full of twinkling, winking stars and a moon so big and bright I felt as though I could reach out and stroke it with my fingertips.

We sat there, reflecting, sharing memories and family stories, taking comfort in their familiarity. Feeling relaxed and peaceful, I recounted my conversation with Skeeter about our unfinished plot to communicate and our failure to agree on a signal in time. As I stared up at the sky, I was suddenly inspired, and I smiled as I said, "I know, I'll just make up a signal myself, right now." After all, we felt Skeeter's presence, and there was no reason to believe he wouldn't hear my words. I looked up and told him, "Okay, Skeeter, if we see a falling star in the next ten minutes, then we'll know it's you, telling us that all is truly well."

We looked at each other and resumed our conversation, as before. Within moments, Lisa's eyes widened and she pointed excitedly toward the sky, crying, "Look, look!"

We all turned our faces upward and there, streaking across the Texas night, was the biggest, brightest, and most beautiful shooting star I have ever seen.

We watched the star burn itself out, then turned to each other, its reflection still there in one another's eyes. The wonder of that moment and the peace it brought to us will stay with us always, right there in our hearts with Skeeter.

—*M. Sissy Clark*

Comment

A miracle comes to us in many different ways. Sometimes it is discreet, almost imperceptible, while at other times, when we need it badly enough, it is blazed across the skies.

*D*awn came to school one morning and delivered to me what was, for her, tragic news.

The "authorities," she said, were forcing her to transfer to a different school. She would be leaving my fourth-grade class soon. She, her mom, and her brothers had been homeless and were living in a hotel. Bureaucrats managed their lives now, and bureaucrats had decreed that she leave the comforting confines of the school.

Dawn had been a difficult student from the start. She was extremely distractible, restless, and somewhat of a bully to her peers. In my thirty-year teaching career, she was the only student I ever had who would work only if she were sitting at my desk rather than hers. Since that strategy succeeded and succeeded well, I allowed her that special liberty. I was just beginning to make significant headway with her when she announced the surprising news of her sudden transfer.

At the beginning of the school year, the class I had was the kind that makes a teacher long for Ritalin to be piped into the air vents! Many of the kids seemed to have attention problems and great difficulty staying focused. In the past, I had devised several tactics in working with this type of student that proved ultimately effective, but the beginning was invariably frustrating . . . and hard.

When Dawn first said that she was leaving, I had, to be honest, mixed feelings. In truth, I knew how well she was doing with me and how content she felt in my class. We also had a great rapport with each other. But this was such an unfocused group that one less attention problem in the class would actually be a relief.

Dawn, however, expressed such sadness about her imminent departure that I was finally won over by her tremendous need to remain. I asked the class to pray collectively to whatever power each child chose, in order to enable her to stay. I, too, prayed. Despite our sincere prayers, however, Dawn was forced to leave the school during the third week of October. From time to time, she returned to the class to visit. She later confided to me that she had been miserable in her new school.

The following year, I was transferred to a different school and a brand-new grade—fifth. I thought about Dawn. I had not had the opportunity to tell her about my transfer, and she had no way of knowing where I was teaching now. She would not be able to visit me, I knew, because she did not know where I was. All that would be left would be her memory.

But, in the third week of October, while I was busy teaching my class, I suddenly looked up and noticed Dawn at my door, standing next to the school guidance counselor.

"You have a new student," he said.

Apparently, when Dawn had been transferred again—this time to the very school that *I* had been transferred to myself—she had met with the guidance teacher for placement counseling. He told me that when she had seen my name on the list of teachers, she became very excited and begged him to put her in my class.

Dawn's reappearance in my life gave me mixed emotions. I was thrilled to see her, but I knew the kind of work I had ahead of me dealing with her attention problem and social skills. I remembered well the difficulty I had experienced the previous year in working with the overwhelming challenges she presented. But I couldn't help but be in awe of the coincidence that had restored her to my care.

For it had been precisely a year ago—the third week of October—that she had been taken *out* of my class. Exactly one year later—during the same time period—she had been mysteriously and unaccountably brought back to me in a different school and in a different grade.

I called her mother that night to marvel over the incredible coincidence. She disclosed that both she and Dawn had prayed for this exact scenario to occur: that Dawn somehow, some way, would miraculously be led to my class.

But how did it happen that Dawn had been transferred *again?* And how had she ended up in *my school?*

Dawn told me that she had moved in with her grandmother, who lived in a different school district. The schoolchildren on her new block just happened to be assigned to my school.

What were the chances of Dawn relocating to a new neighborhood and changing to a new school—the very school to which I had been transferred? How had it happened that after teaching fourth grade, I had suddenly been reassigned to fifth? And what was the likelihood that she would show up on the exact same week she had left my care precisely one year before?

Dawn ended up having a great school year, both academically and socially. Our phenomenal teacher–student relationship became even better, and Dawn blossomed. I really love this child and her family.

Another interesting coincidence occurred this year, now that Dawn is in sixth grade. I was moved to a room on the floor above, which just happens to be directly across from the very room that Dawn is assigned to this year! We get to talk and give each other a hug every time we pass in the hall. And Dawn can visit me anytime because my room is just a few short feet away from hers.

—*Chana-Chaya Bailey*

$\mathcal{A}$ *few* weeks after my husband passed away, in December 1987, I undertook the painful task of going through his papers. I sat down one day and separated the papers that still had significance from the old letters, certificates, photographs and so on that had lost all meaning with his passing. The former I restored to their place on the closet shelf; the latter I discarded.

Throughout the day, memories of my husband flooded my consciousness. It had been hard for me to fall asleep that night, but, finally, towards midnight, I fell into a deep slumber. Suddenly I was awakened by a loud thud, as though something heavy had fallen. With difficulty I roused myself and made the rounds of the rooms. Everything seemed to be in order, so I went back to sleep.

By morning I had all but forgotten the incident. But then I noticed a bare spot on the wall. A self-portrait of my husband, a professional artist, had fallen behind an armchair. The cord that had held it in place for the past twenty-five years had frayed, sending the portrait to the floor and awakening me on that special night of intense communion with his memory. I was startled by the coincidence, but promptly replaced the cord and put the picture back in its usual place.

Eight years passed. In August 1996 my apartment was burglarized while I was away, and the burglars emptied the contents of my closets onto the floor. Tears welled up in my eyes when I came home and saw the mess. Family documents, my children's drawings, souvenirs dating back over forty years, letters, photographs, were all scrambled together. It took me a full day to restore some semblance of order. As I lovingly examined memories of our courtship and early years of marriage—tender letters and poems, a pressed rose—the years seemed to fall away.

That night my dreams were of my husband. However, they were interrupted in the middle of the night by a loud thud. The same scenario that had taken place eight years ago replayed itself. A superficial inspection showed nothing amiss, and I went back to bed. In the morning I discovered that the frame of my husband's self-portrait was empty. It was still hanging on the wall, but the painting itself had somehow slipped out and crashed to the floor.

—Rosalie E. Moriah

Comment

Lodged in the physical objects we create is a remnant of ourselves, and sometimes that remnant seeks a voice.

Small Miracles of Love & Friendship

I was never afraid of people or dogs. When the Nazis entered my life, I became afraid of people. Before then, my family lived in a spacious apartment in Warsaw. My father, an electrical engineer, operated a successful small appliance factory. We had all the comforts of family life. Since I had no brothers or sisters, my father gave me a most loyal, loving and obedient friend to keep me company while he and mother were at work.

He was a male terrier, with black eyes trustingly peeking through gray fur, and answering to "Motek." I played with him, teased him, bathed him and fed him. Sometimes, after playing and rough-housing, Motek became excited and uncontrollable. I would talk to him, and my soft low voice seemed to get through and calm him. As a matter of fact, people used to say that my voice could quell an erupting volcano.

After the Germans came, we were forced to live in the Warsaw ghetto in very tight quarters, but Motek came with us. He was considered a member of the family.

Three years later, everything had changed. The Nazis murdered my father in the ghetto, my mother starved to death in a slave labor camp, Motek was shot by the Germans and the ghetto was burned to the ground.

I was transported to the infamous Majdanek death camp, near Lublin. Very few survived its gas chambers, which, as in Auschwitz, operated day and night. Soon after my arrival in the summer of 1943, I was unfortunate enough to be near a minor altercation among several prisoners. The tower guards fired into the group, and I was hit. A bullet passed through my right thigh.

At Majdanek, it was customary to kill sick and wounded inmates. The doctor who was called to the scene questioned me about the incident. I told him the facts and emphasized my innocent involvement. He thought for a moment and told me he would treat me at the clinic because he liked the sound of my voice.

I recovered just in time to be placed on the transfer list to the slave labor camp at Skarzynsko-Kamienna, also near Lublin, on the railway line to Treblinka. When I arrived, I was just 18 and, compared to others, was considered able-bodied for work. I was assigned the job of filling 20 mm. cartridge shells with explosives.

The Camp Kommandant was a tough SS officer who ruled with an iron fist. His men patrolled the area with vicious guard dogs to prevent resistance or escape. Living conditions were dreadful, food was scarce, facilities primitive, and hopeless despair dominated the prisoners. No one had a friend, except for me. Surprisingly, I shared him with the ruthless SS Kommandant.

I didn't know his name, but I called him "Kelev," Hebrew for dog. He was the only thing that seemed to bring an occasional smile to the hard face of the Kommandant. Kelev was a magnificent Great Dane, with smooth black and white fur contoured by every muscle into a picture of strength and power. His dark eyes were sad and penetrating. He had free run of the camp and sniffed and barked at the grimy prisoners. He frightened and terrorized them, but not me. I talked to him, petted him, played with him, and calmed him, and we became friends. The guards smiled tolerantly at the sight of the skinny girl communicating with the Kommandant's pet. They were more lenient and looked aside when I occasionally stood by as the dog was being fed. They may not have been so tolerant had they caught me helping myself to some of the dog food—it was a delicacy compared to what I had to eat. It meant so much to me to have someone to talk to, to care for, to caress, to be snuggled up against and to be slobbered over. It camouflaged my feeling of hopelessness.

One morning, after I had been in Skarzynsko-Kamienna about eleven months, we were ordered to assemble for "parade." I had survived several during the year. The prisoners were lined up and marched past a group of SS officers. The Kommandant stood in the background and observed the proceedings. Those who appeared healthy were motioned to one side to be shipped to factories which had requisitioned additional laborers, and those who looked too ill to work were ordered to the other side, to be shot.

By that time I had contracted typhoid, had lost my hair, and, at age 19, weighed less than 80 pounds. I was sent to join the condemned. Suddenly, I heard a yip and a bark. I looked up to see the Great Dane move away from the Kommandant, walk slowly, carefully, powerfully and majestically toward me, his eyes never leaving mine. His tail swung in a deliberate, even beat like a metronome as he came alongside me to be caressed.

I bent over, smiled at him, talked to him, stroked his head and back, rubbed his sides, and softly said my farewell. He licked my bony hand. It would probably be the last act of affection I would ever receive—and that from a dog. Much to my surprise, the Kommandant suddenly called to one of the officers, motioned toward me, and I was ordered to leave the group of the dead and join that of the living. Kelev walked beside me, close to my bony legs, as I took my place among the lucky ones.

A few days later, I was transported to a munitions factory in the Buchenwald Concentration Camp complex near Leipzig. Ill as I was, I worked hard to survive. When the Red Army overran the area and liberated me nine months later, I was all skin and bones. But I was alive!

Today, I live in Israel, the only place in which I feel safe. It is not often that I think back to the horrible days of my youth. But sometimes when I sit on my balcony and watch children play or walk with their dogs, I remember Kelev. At first he represented companionship and hope. In the end, he represented life itself—my life.

—*Ester Milshstein*

Finding himself becoming increasingly consumed by the Internet, Ron Elkins had resolved, in a moment of introspection, to avoid his computer altogether. "Wasting too much time on the Web," he concluded.

He had stuck by his resolution for two months and he was proud he could resist the Web's allure, despite its apparent advantages.

One of those advantages had been the many new friends he had met online. Dave, a warm-hearted, generous-spirited man who helped various people with their problems, was among this group of online friends. He had been instrumental in helping Ron, when he had been going through a bad time.

Dave had committed suicide two months before. No one knew why. Ron often thought about how much Dave had helped him, and he still mourned him. Maybe this sadness contributed to his decision to shun the Internet.

But in July 1997, in a coffeehouse that featured four terminals hooked up to America Online, the computer beckoned.

Ron missed his friend dearly and longed to find someone online who had known Dave, too, and to see if anyone understood why he would kill himself. While it was true that Dave was divorced, had battled many

personal difficulties, and was a member of AA, he
seemed to be handling things well. He was such a rock
for so many people; why couldn't he be a rock for
himself? Ron just had to know. He looked at the
computers in the coffeehouse and his hard-won
resistance crumbled.

Three of the four computers in the coffeehouse were
not in use, so Ron made a beeline for one. He logged on
to America Online and went searching for any "buddies
online" with whom he had chatted in the past. He
pulled up one name, read the profile, and then
discarded it. He pulled up another name, pored over
the profile, and noted that it read: "Friend of Bill W."
Here he stopped.

Ron knew that "Bill W." was the founder of "AA"—
Alcoholics Anonymous, the recovery organization. He
also knew that Dave had been a member of this group
and had been working the "Sixth Step" prior to his
death. Maybe this anonymous guy who was online right
now by some slim chance knew his friend.

"May I ask you a question?" Ron typed into the
computer.

"Yes, you may," the anonymous person replied
immediately.

"Did you know 'BIDASK DAVE' (Dave's user
name), otherwise known as Dave V?" Ron asked.

"I knew Dave very well," came the reply.

Ron was shocked that out of millions of people online, he had found someone by chance who did indeed know Dave.

"May I ask you another question?" he typed.

And then there was no reply.

"Hello, are you there?" Ron typed. He was perplexed. Why was the "buddy" not responding? A computer malfunction?

He typed his message in again: "Are you there? Did you know Dave V?"

Still no answer. Ron couldn't understand it. He sat in his chair, puzzled.

A minute later, a stranger approached him and asked: "How did *you* know Dave?"

Of all the anonymous millions of people in the United States who use America Online, Ron had just sent an "instant message" to the guy using the computer at the other end of the same coffeehouse!

Without exchanging names or making formal introductions, the two immediately launched into an animated discussion about Dave, swapping stories of how they had each met him, and of what he had meant to them both. Then the stranger excused himself for a minute, returned with a cappuccino, and said enigmatically: "I *know* you, you *know* me, and I *know* your wife."

Ron was dumbfounded. "You know me? You know my wife?" he repeated.

The stranger nodded and said emphatically, "Yes, I know your wife Diane very well."

Ron looked shocked. He did not recognize the man in front of him, and he never forgot a face. "Who *are* you?" he asked nervously.

The man revealed that he was Mark, a childhood friend of Ron's wife, a friend who shared much of her history. He had been one of the few intimates whom Diane had invited to their wedding who hadn't shown up on that important day of her life. He hadn't called afterwards, either to explain or to apologize. Diane had felt so hurt and rejected by his no-show that she hadn't talked to Mark since. Five years later, when she and Ron had their first baby, her old friend Mark had phoned with congratulations. His call had shocked and upset Diane. It brought back all the memories of what he had done.

Mark made many attempts to patch things up, but Ron's wife could neither forgive nor forget. She asked Ron to call Mark and tell him to leave her alone. To protect his wife from further distress, Ron had actually gone to the man's place of work and warned him to never contact his wife again. The friend had then stopped calling Diane, and neither of them had ever seen or heard from him again.

Now, fifteen years later, Ron was in the coffeehouse, companionably sharing drinks with the very man who had hurt his wife so badly and whom he had threatened in turn!

As they sat at the table, Mark finally confessed the secret he had been hiding all these years. He had been unable to attend their wedding because he had been thoroughly and utterly drunk at the time, unable to even pull himself out of bed. He had not called because he felt so horrible and ashamed about missing his childhood friend's wedding. He was in his twenties at the time, with no confidant and no one to help him. He had not shared his serious drinking problem with a single soul. No one had ever known the truth, not even his closest friends.

Mark disclosed that he missed Diane terribly. Not a day went by that he didn't think of her. He had even kept her picture taped to his mirror all these years.

When Ron heard the confession, he felt partly happy, partly sad.

Sad that his wife's childhood friend had had such a terrible problem and had hidden it and struggled with it for so many years alone. Sad that such a beautiful friendship had needlessly ended. And sad that there had been so many lost years.

The happiness that filled Ron, however, came from the certain knowledge that once his wife understood what had really happened on their wedding day, she would forgive her friend. The relationship that had meant so much to both would be restored.

The next morning, Ron recounted to his wife the odd coincidence that had brought him to her old friend and explained the circumstances that had kept Mark from attending their wedding. His wife was shocked to learn the truth about her old friend and upset that he had been unable to confide in her and that she had misunderstood his intentions all this time.

Three weeks later, they all met for dinner. When Diane and Mark saw each other after twenty years' time, they both burst into tears, simultaneously.

It was the right time for them to meet once again, and the friendship has picked up right where it left off.

—Ronald Elkins

❧

Comment
Time, space, and synchronicity are all "virtual realities" in God's world.

"**W**here's my boat?" cried Dennis Bennetts, as he stood at the edge of the clear, blue Australian waters, staring incredulously into the calm, empty ocean. Just moments before, he had been loading his beloved vessel, *The Classic*, in preparation for a much-anticipated fishing trip. But now his prized boat was nowhere to be seen. "*The Classic* is missing from the dock—someone must have let it loose!" he moaned in despair. Scanning the vast body of water before him, Dennis realized that the craft that had brought him years of memories and enjoyment was probably now drifting off toward the horizon, never to be seen again.

Six months later and five thousand miles away, fellow Australian Kathy Brennan and her boyfriend, Kregg, were backpacking their way through Africa. The guidebook warned against visiting Mozambique because of a civil war in that country. But when the couple reached Swaziland, they met travelers who assured them that Mozambique was indeed safe, and the two decided to venture through that country after all.

Because many tourists had been warned against traveling through this area, however, Kathy and Kregg stood out in each town they visited. In one particular village, while the couple relaxed under the wide shade of a tree, taking shelter from the bright African sun, two young boys ran eagerly toward them. "Look!" the boys exclaimed, excited to make contact with the exotic foreigners. "We found a paper . . . written in your language . . . inside a boat, at the shore! Come, look!" The couple followed the boys to the edge of the ocean, where they saw a beautiful boat, lazily lapping against the shore. The boat looked well-maintained, but it was empty.

Kathy gingerly stepped into the craft and began leafing through papers she found inside. Her heart skipped a beat as she recognized familiar names and addresses. Then her eyes opened wide in disbelief. "Kregg!" she called excitedly. "You've got to see this — you won't believe it!"

Kregg rushed to her side, in time to share in her amazement. "Dennis Bennetts!" she cried. "This boat belongs to Dennis Bennetts! Kregg . . . Dennis is my next-door neighbor in Australia!"

There stood Kathy, on the edge of the water in a remote corner of Africa, on a small boat that had somehow traveled five thousand miles on its own. Later oceanographers explained that currents in the Indian Ocean, coupled with strong winds, had buffeted *The Classic* along at a rate of 40 miles a day until, six months later, it completed its incredible journey to Africa — to land at Kathy and Kregg's feet.

Kathy ran to make a call.

"I've got your boat, neighbor."

I couldn't believe my ears. My soon-to-be-ex-husband told me that he had my "Fourth Step Inventory," just about the most personal thing I had ever written in my life, and was passing out copies to parents and students in the school in which I was a teacher.

I was working a twelve-step program called "Overeaters Anonymous," fashioned after the original recovery organization, Alcoholics Anonymous. It is a program of fellowship in which we are no longer alone. The program suggests twelve steps as a means to recovery.

The Fourth Step advises us to "make a fearless and searching moral inventory of ourselves." It is suggested that we "be fearless and thorough from the very start" and that "the results are nil until we let go absolutely." I was told that this was to be a list of everything I had ever done in my life that I felt the slightest bit guilty for. Also, in case I didn't already have enough to feel guilty about, there were guidelines that gave additional ideas of things to put in that I might not even have thought of.

I was in the process of doing this inventory with a rigorous honesty and fearlessness as instructed. Since I had felt guilty even for fantasizing something, I had included those fantasies in the inventory. I wanted to come out of this step totally cleansed, so if I even thought of something I wrote it down.

At the time this inventory writing was going on, I was in the process of divorcing an abusive husband. I added to this inventory daily and because of the myriad of fantasies that usually plagued my brain, the inventory was quite long. I hid it each day in my clothing closet, under a pile of blankets and pillows.

On a particular Friday afternoon, I was scheduled to be the speaker for a well-attended OA meeting in Oceanside, New York. After one has worked the steps and the tools of the program successfully, one is asked to "give back" to the members by sharing personal experience, strength, and hope with the group.

It was a few hours before the scheduled speaking engagement that my soon-to-be-ex told me that he had my inventory and had made copies of it. He said he had not only gone to the school where I was a teacher and passed it out to parents, but he was also going to use it in court to get the children away from me. He said he didn't want them, but he didn't want me to have them either.

I am sure I don't have to explain to anyone how I felt. Here I was doing what I felt was following a spiritual path and then this! How could it be? I made a few frenzied calls to friends in the program and soon decided that it would all work out for the best. I said optimistically to one friend: "Given the good luck that I anticipate, I bet that the judge in the case will turn out to be an AA member himself! This judge will see my husband using the program against me and will throw him out of court or something like that!" I decided that God hadn't brought me this far to drop me on my face.

I let go of the huge betrayal in my head and heart and went that afternoon to speak at the meeting. I told the story of my past and my present and of course included what had happened with my inventory and how the judge would probably throw my husband out of court. I also mentioned that my children were being abused by my husband.

After the meeting, one of the many people who came up to talk to me was an elderly woman crying about how her growing-up years had been so much like mine.

My husband had hired a well-known attorney. *My* attorney was hired at the advice of a friend who said she had received a good settlement because her husband's own attorney wasn't too swift. At the time, I was in my twenties and oblivious to the fact that it was important to get a sharp attorney. I had no idea that my ex would be aware of such a thing either. I was not even aware that my lawyer was no match for this high-priced shark.

The Sunday immediately following the OA meeting, I got a phone call from my husband's lawyer. I told him that my husband was not at home.

"Did you speak in Oceanside on Friday afternoon?" he asked.

I felt panic rise up inside of me. There were so many people at the meeting, listening to me. Could my husband's lawyer have been one of them? I was horrified at the thought of that possibility. But when he said that his mother had heard me and that her story was so similar to mine that she repeated it to him, I admitted that indeed it was I who had spoken there. He said that it was only because she had told him that the lawyer had the inventory of the speaker, that he knew that the speaker was me.

"After all," he added, "how many lawyers have the inventory of their client's wife?"

He then asked if it were true that my children were being abused. He said that if I had told him in his office, he would not have believed me.

"But," he remarked, "you said it at an OA meeting and at an OA meeting, you do not lie."

In the course of the conversation, he even asked if when the divorce was finalized, I would be his sponsor in the program! We talked and he told me that before this, he had had every intention of torturing me in this divorce process and making me suffer until I was ready to settle for nothing. But he was now going to call my lawyer at home right away, and by tomorrow morning I would have a fair agreement.

And so he did!

What was supposed to be a torturous, drawn-out divorce was now quick, fair, and simple.

How ironic. The worst thing about this divorce process turned out to be the very thing that saved me. Had my ex-husband not given his lawyer my Fourth

Step inventory, the lawyer would not have known that the woman who touched his mother's heart was me, and he would not have come to my aid. Rather, he would have caused me great suffering.

From the get-go, it looked as if I were clearly doomed. It was my husband who had the celebrated attorney and the money to pay. He had my inventory. He didn't care if he got the kids. Everything appeared to be against me.

Somehow my higher power worked it out. I had fantasized that it would be the judge who would figuratively slap my husband down. But I got something even better. I didn't even have to go before a judge. And it was my husband's own lawyer who helped me. My wildest imagination could not have dreamed up anything this amazing.

How many times have I heard devastating news only to find out later how truly beneficial it really was?

How many times have things looked so hopeless, only to turn out to be wonderful instead?

With each time I learn this lesson, I become more in awe of what God can do and even more in awe of what He actually does.

—Chana Chaya Bailey

It's a love story not made *for* television, but made possible *by* television.

New Yorker Arlene DeCrenza, who hadn't seen her "first love" for twenty-two years and had unsuccessfully hunted for him in the past, turned on the television one night and had the shock of her life.

An ABC Eyewitness News team had flown down to Florida in February 1998 for on-the-spot reportage, after killer tornadoes had swept through the Sunshine State. Residents from Kissimmee were being randomly interviewed for their reactions to the devastation, and among them was a very familiar face.

Arlene, divorced and living in Westchester County, couldn't believe that her first love, Gene Mershell, whom she had failed to find six years before during an extensive, but alas, fruitless search, was on the screen, right in front of her. After the broadcast, Arlene excitedly contacted Eyewitness News in New York, who reunited her with Gene, also divorced, on the program via satellite.

"I've missed you," he said shyly.

"I've missed you too," she confessed.

And then she scolded, "Why haven't you called?"

The two first met when they were seventeen, when he was a counselor at a camp where her family vacationed.

After the broadcast, they began dating again, and Gene flew to New York to court Arlene in earnest. Six months later—on August 23, 1998—they said "I do" at a beautiful wedding in Briarcliff Manor, New York.

The ABC Eyewitness News team was invited.

In fact, said reporter Martin Solis, ABC was there for all the major milestones of this not-so-minor miracle.

"We were there when they first reestablished contact," he noted, "and we reported on the wedding as well.

"The only landmark event that we were not allowed to cover was the honeymoon."

Comment

As long as we keep the embers of our desires burning brightly, not days, nor months, nor years can ever extinguish its flames.

Because my father, Michael, was an artist, I've enjoyed a life of wonderful surprises. Any day can bring a letter from someone who owns one of his paintings and wants to know more about him. Any visit to an art gallery can lead to the discovery of a canvas I've never seen before.

I suppose there must be hundreds of undiscovered paintings waiting to burst into my life in unexpected ways, and I can hardly express the emotions I feel when they do. My dad died in 1971, yet when I discover a painting for the first time, I almost believe he has sent it to me from "out there" somewhere.

Of course, it would be an exaggeration to classify the discovery of every painting as a coincidence. When someone owns one of my dad's paintings and looks me up, that's a fairly straightforward process—even though it delights and surprises me.

Yet the way some paintings have emerged through happenstance goes beyond simple routine and edges into the remarkable. Let me tell you about two such interesting coincidences—and one so extraordinary that it truly strains credibility.

Once, when I was attending the opening of a show about mural activity in New Jersey in the 1930s (my dad, Michael Lenson, was head of the New Jersey mural division of the Federal Art Project/WPA in those years), I was introduced to Marlene Park, the distinguished art historian. When she heard my name, her eyes lit up. Just days earlier, the Smithsonian Institution had called her, wanting information about my dad. Two of his murals had turned up in the lobby of an apartment house in the Bronx, and the owner of the building had contacted the Smithsonian to ask whether they had any value. Those murals now reside in the collection of the Wolfsonian Institution in Florida.

Another time, I was attending an exhibition at the Midtown Galleries in New York. I was elated to meet the legendary Mary Gruskin, who founded that gallery in the mid-1930s with her husband, John. Ms. Gruskin said to me, "Oh, yes, Michael Lenson"—then led me into the back room and showed me photographs of two of my father's paintings that had been in her gallery in the 1930s. I had never seen those paintings before, but I own them today.

Those are interesting "long-shot" serendipities, to be sure, but they can't compare to this one, which requires a little background information.

In 1928, my father won the most prestigious art prize of the day—the $10,000 Paris Prize, offered by the Chaloner Foundation. That was an awful lot of money back then—it's a tidy sum today. My dad, who sorted mail in the Post Office to pay for his studies at the National Academy of Design, was suddenly on his way to four years of study in Paris, London, and Spain. As he later wrote, "All my relatives who saw me as a no-good deficit to the family were suddenly on the wharf, waving good-bye."

During his years abroad—the years in Paris, especially—he created some extraordinary paintings. He was very much under the influence of Titian and the many old masters whose works he studied at the Louvre. Our family owned very few of his paintings from those years. Some had been left behind in Europe. Others had been sold after his return.

But by far the most remarkable paintings from the years 1928 through 1932 had passed into the collection of a woman named Leila Livian, a prominent singing teacher of the day. Soon after my father returned to New York in 1932, he traded paintings for lessons. And those remarkable paintings were "out there" somewhere, waiting to be found.

So in the early 1980s, I resolved to try to find them. It would be difficult, since I knew from my mother that Leila Livian had passed away many years before. However, my mother also knew that Leila Livian had been married to a man named Nathaniel Ratner. That was not an awful lot to go on, but enough for an amateur detective like me. So I was off and running in my search for him.

I turned first to my favorite people-finding book, the Manhattan phone book. I had no idea where Nathaniel Ratner lived—it might have been anywhere from Maine to California—but I cracked open the directory and looked up "Ratner."

Of course, there were many Ratners listed in New York. I found no Nathaniel listed, but I did find an "N. Ratner." So I picked up the phone and dialed. In a few moments, a woman answered.

I still remember the conversation vividly.

"Hello," I said. "I am trying to reach Mr. Nathaniel Ratner. I am sorry to bother you if this is not his home, but if it is, I wonder if I could speak with him."

"Well," the woman answered, after thinking a moment, "I'm sorry that I do not know a Nathaniel Ratner. May I ask what this is in reference to?"

I explained that I was trying to locate some paintings that were owned by Nathaniel Ratner.

"Well," she answered, "if you like, I could ask around my husband's family to see whether he is related to us. Out of curiosity, could you tell me a little about the paintings you are looking for?"

"My father was a painter named Michael Lenson," I said, then went on to explain a little about who my father was and what his paintings were like.

"I don't know Nathaniel Ratner," she said with a laugh, "but I do own a drawing by your father!"

She then went on to tell me a remarkable story.

"When I was a girl, I went to a summer camp in Pennsylvania. It must have been sometime around 1916. One of the counselors was a wildly handsome teenage boy. We girls were all absolutely taken with him. And he made absolutely extraordinary drawings of many of us. Not camper caricatures, mind you, but very revealing and beautiful drawings. . . . I still cherish the one your father did of *me*."

So there was no overlooking the fact that dialing what was essentially a wrong number in a city of eight million people had located one of my father's works, without even trying. And a very unusual work, at that—a drawing from the very start of his life, something I would not even have known to look for.

Now, you're probably wondering whether I found Nathaniel Ratner and the missing works. I did, through an orderly process of contacting a rather famous soprano who had also studied with Leila Livian. This woman knew just where to find Nathaniel Ratner and the paintings I was looking for, which were well worth the search. Best of all, Nat's become a great friend and he adores the paintings. Finding a good friend was the best surprise of all.

But I often return in my mind to that "wrong number" coincidence. And when I do, I always hear my father's voice saying to me, "Well, Bar', as long as you were looking anyway, I thought maybe there was another little something you might want to know about too."

—*Barry Lenson*

✎

Comment

To allow passion to drive you to your goal, stash gut consciousness away, put limited thinking aside and risk.

*I*n Israel, where fertile land is at a premium and there are no fields for grazing cattle, beef is a scarce commodity and must be imported from South America. Much of Israel's beef comes in fact from Paraguay, and it was to that country that three Israeli rabbi-butchers regularly traveled. They worked there in an enormous slaughterhouse that allowed them to slaughter cattle according to Jewish law, thus providing Israel's citizens with kosher meat. They had worked in the same slaughterhouse for three years, and despite the hazards of the place—its sheer size, the treacherous machinery, the formidable proportions of the cattle— they felt safe.

One day, however, something untoward happened. Inspecting some meat inside an enormous freezer, the rabbis were startled by the sound of a thunderous clang as the massive freezer door suddenly slammed shut behind them, imprisoning them inside.

They stared at each other in horror. They shouted for help. They pounded vigorously on the door. But no one responded. Neither their voices nor their noisy efforts seemed to be reaching a single ear.

"Surely someone will pass by soon and hear our banging and thumping," one rabbi reassured the others.

"Of course!" another answered heartily. "Someone is bound to find us soon enough."

But no one did.

Hours passed. The rabbis had shouted and thumped and pounded endlessly, but not a soul had heard their cries.

Overcome by lack of oxygen and the freezing temperatures, the rabbis grew weak. Their voices became fainter as their energy slowly seeped away. Their initial optimism faded. Checking their watches, they realized that it was closing time at the massive plant. With this realization, all hope died.

They talked sorrowfully about the wives and children they would be leaving behind. They pulled out the miniature Psalms they always carried in their pockets and began to prepare for the worst. A strange calm descended on them. They had already accepted their fate.

Outside the slaughterhouse, Emilio, the manager, was grappling with the padlock as he prepared to secure the building for the night. As was his custom, prior to locking up, he had walked through the plant to ensure that there were no stragglers left behind and, seeing none, had shut the facility down. Walking toward the parking lot he passed the security guard, Emilio was surprised to see Golya, the security guard, standing at his usual post.

"Golya!" he exclaimed. "Weren't you supposed to be starting your vacation today?"

"Indeed I was, sir," Golya replied, "but at the last minute, my temporary replacement called in sick.

Personnel asked if I could do them a favor and stay one more day. The new guy will start tomorrow instead, and then I'm off!"

"Well, have a good one!" Emilio said heartily, as he waved good-bye and headed to his car.

"Sir!" the guard called after him uneasily, "you're not leaving for the night, are you?"

Emilio was startled by the query. Golya had never questioned him like this before.

"Why, yes, Golya," he replied. "Of course I am locking up for the night. It's way past closing time."

"But sir," Golya said anxiously, "I'm quite sure that there are some people inside."

"What are you talking about, Golya?" Emilio said. "I checked the plant myself, as I always do, every night. Everyone's gone."

"Please, sir, I'm quite sure. Please check again."

Emilio thought that Golya was acting strangely, but he was a conscientious, dependable man who had never given him pause or trouble. To humor him, Emilio backtracked to the slaughterhouse and checked it thoroughly a second time. And once again, he saw nothing and no one.

Returning to the security checkpoint, Emilio reassured Golya. "Everything's fine. There's no one inside."

Golya, usually a timid man, was uncharacteristically forceful.

"Everything's *not* fine, sir. I am sure there are some people inside. Please check again."

Emilio studied Golya with interest. Golya had never been so strong or assertive before, not in all the years he had known him. His behavior was *so* odd.

"Please, sir!" Golya begged.

Once again, Emilio returned to the slaughterhouse, walked through it carefully, and reassured himself that despite Golya's misgivings, nothing was amiss.

But such assurances did not soothe the by-now-intractable Golya.

"I am telling you there are people inside!" he insisted loudly.

Emilio was getting annoyed. What was the matter with the security guard? "Look, Golya, this is getting ridiculous! I've checked three times."

"Then let me go with you, sir, and help you check again!" Golya pressed.

Golya was acting so strangely that Emilio was at a loss as to what to do. Finally, he succumbed to Golya's pleas. "Okay, come along," he said.

Golya's search was more thorough than Emilio's. He inspected closets, checked the floors, hunched down next to massive machines to see if someone was trapped underneath. The manager was utterly baffled by the security guard's strange behavior. *Was he out of his mind?*

Then they advanced toward the freezer, which Emilio had bypassed before.

"That's it!" shouted Golya with conviction as he flung open the door in triumph. Inside, blue and unconscious, lay the three rabbis.

"But how did you know?" Emilio asked Golya later, long after the excitement had subsided and the rabbis had been rushed to the hospital, where they were resuscitated.

Golya explained.

"These rabbis have been coming here for three years. Every time they come, they come over to talk with me. When they arrive in the morning, they always stop and say: 'Hi, Golya, good morning, how are you, how's your family, how's work going, have a good day, see you later.' When they leave in the evening, it's the same thing. They always stop for a few last words. 'So, Golya,' they say, 'how did your day go? Anything exciting happen? What's for supper?' and so on. They always make me feel like I'm important, like I count. And they've been doing this for three years straight. And even if I'm gone from my post for a minute just as they are about to leave, they wait until I'm back to say good-bye. All these years, it's never happened once that they didn't make sure to wish me good night before they left the plant.

"Sir," Golya continued, "when you came out of the building and locked up for the night, I was worried. 'Golya,' I said to myself, 'for three years those rabbis have stopped to say goodnight to you without fail. Why should tonight be different?' So I knew that something must be terribly wrong," he concluded, "and that they must be trapped somewhere inside."

⁓⁓⁓

Comment
The dance of return has many strange steps.

I was thirty-one years old this past January, when I answered the door to two policemen who informed me that my husband had been killed instantly in a horrible car accident.

Although he was wearing a seat belt, my husband had either fallen asleep or had missed the bend in the road. His truck had slid off the highway into a hole and smashed into a tree. He had been crushed to death.

Compounding the horror of this news was the sudden realization that the life insurance premiums had not been paid, and our policy had lapsed. Apparently, when we had thought we were replacing one policy with another, we had unknowingly canceled both. All these months, we had been unaware of this fatal error, never realizing that the money was no longer being automatically deducted from our account.

I was a teacher, making less than $30,000 a year, and I was living in a home with a $900-per-month mortgage. I was paying $360 a month in day care expenses and had a car payment of $340 a month. These bills alone far exceeded my income. In addition, I was repaying a college loan, had some credit card debt, and was now also faced with a $7,000 funeral bill. I had no idea how I was going to continue paying the bills.

Miraculously, over the course of the next few months, I found myself consistently "reimbursed" to the exact dollar amount for every sizable check I needed to write. Every seen and unforeseen expense was time and again mysteriously returned to me.

This began with the selling of my home. I was able to sell it immediately, but unable to move until I made the arrangements to have a mobile home placed on my brother's property. This would take three months, which meant that I needed to be able to continue paying my current mortgage until I was able to move. As I opened the many condolence cards I had received, I felt tremendous relief and deep gratitude well up inside of me. In heartwarming displays of friendship and love, many people had placed money inside the condolence cards, and I understood then that these friends would help with the house payments. The money netted by the first group of condolence cards amounted to $2,700—the exact amount of money I needed to make three months' worth of mortgage payments!

The day I purchased my mobile home, I wrote out a check for the $500 deposit. That evening, as I was opening my mail, I found an anonymous money order made out to me in the amount of $500. A typed note accompanying the gift said: *"I was a friend of Aaron's* (my husband). *I hope this helps."*

A month later, as I was paying my bills, I wrote out my first mortgage payment. That evening, my mother-in-law stopped by with a condolence card from her coworkers. In the card was a check for the exact amount of the mortgage check I had just written.

Just recently, I was struggling with a decision about whether to keep my son in an overcrowded public school or to transfer him instead to a private school with smaller class sizes. The cost was an obvious concern. I was informed by the school that the cost for kindergarten was $617. During the week that I was weighing this decision, I received a reimbursement check from my automobile insurance for a policy I had mistakenly been paying on the vehicle involved in the accident. The check was in the amount of $555. Days after receiving the check, the private school offered me a sweet deal: If I would pay the school tuition in full, I would pay a discounted amount—$555.

I later found out that due to the fact that my husband was wearing a seatbelt, I was entitled to some money. This amount was exactly the same sum I needed to pay off my car loan.

Then, in an incredibly magnanimous gesture of love and support, my husband's best friend, Marty, stepped forward to pay the funeral bill in full.

Although I'm now "living simply," my bills have been greatly reduced and my son and I have all our needs met. I do have considerably less "stuff" than the $400,000 life insurance policy that lapsed would have provided; however, through this experience I have gained an overwhelming trust in God and peace of mind.

No amount of money in the world could have shown me so clearly that forces beyond our comprehension are at work within our world and that expecting miracles, as I have come to, invites these forces right into our lives.

—Rosemarie J. Brody

❦

Comment

From time to time, we are reminded that money is not merely a medium of secular exchange, but a vehicle for spiritual communication as well.

*I*n 1983, I married into a large Irish Catholic family. Being an only child, I was eager to experience festive holidays with love and all the trimmings. Soon, however, I learned that my husband, Bob, the eldest, and his younger brother, Terry, had had a falling out and remained estranged. Somehow I knew that under all the misunderstanding there was a lot of love, and I longed for them to be "real brothers." While I told myself I was naive, I couldn't shake my hope.

Three years passed. On a bone-chilling Tuesday night in January, Bob and I were unhappily dressing for an unexpected dinner with one of his clients, reluctant to leave our toasty Manhattan apartment to drive an hour to a small New Jersey restaurant.

As we drove, we talked about mediocre food; dutiful, dry conversation; and getting home early.

At least the restaurant is warm, I thought, as we walked into a rather charming dining room. Once we were seated, we relaxed and began to enjoy ourselves. Then my husband saw him.

"*Terry's* here," he said tensely.

My brain swam. "He lives in New Jersey, but not in *this* area," I said. "It's a freezing Tuesday night—what is he doing here? Maybe he won't see us. . . . Vain hope, here he comes."

Terry made Don Rickles look like a fairy godfather, with Bob the brunt of all his barbs. And Bob just laughed uncomfortably.

Mercifully, Terry soon went back to his table, leaving a wake of tension that lasted most of the dinner.

On the way home in the car, ever the optimist, I said to my husband, "I'm sure the power of your love for each other pulled you together. This can't have been a coincidence."

I don't know what he thought, but neither of us was prepared for what happened two months later.

We had been in South America for about a week, had visited a friend of mine in Buenos Aires and were in Rio de Janeiro, breathlessly climbing the endless stairway up to Corcovado, the statue that watches over the harbor. My legs were killing me, so I slowed down and told my husband to go on ahead. When I reached the top, I wasn't disappointed—even though throngs of people were everywhere, the view was everything the travel books had promised. I stood dazzled for a few moments, letting the magic of Rio sweep over me. Then I looked around for Bob.

Instead of Bob, I saw a family lined up to have their pictures taken—my brother-in-law Terry, his wife, her parents, and my three young nephews! *They* had come to South America to see Halley's Comet; *we* had come to see friends and Machu Pichu.

When I caught up with Bob, I learned that he had spotted Terry as well. Bob found his brother and family near the guard rail, about to be photographed by an accommodating stranger. He had put his own camera over his face and had advanced menacingly toward Terry, who was thinking, *Hey, that guy looks like one of the men from our cruise ship. . . . No, actually, that guy looks like Bobbie . . . That guy is Bobbie!"*

The coincidence was so profound that this time the humor was benign and the talk genuinely friendly. My sister-in-law said, "I wish I had these odds at the track!"

I thought, *There are no odds when it comes to love's power.*

That was twelve years ago and the two brothers are truly brothers to this day.

— *Virginia Duffy*

Comment

When love tries to restore its bond, there is no escaping the magnetic field it creates.

*N*ot long ago my wife, Alma, died after nearly fifty-eight years of marriage. She was my partner not only at home but also in my business, serving as listener, advisor, and even an unpaid secretary at times. When I look back on the happiness we shared, I realize ours was a match made in heaven. And I especially remember that day early in our marriage when I received the reassurance that she was meant for me.

Getting to know each other as newlyweds, we were sharing family photos. Alma pointed out different relatives and explained who was who. "This is my grandmother and that's my uncle. . . . " She started to unroll a large group photograph. "I'll have you know I was once at the White House," she bragged.

"When?" I asked. She pointed at the date in the corner of the photo—1928—and I thought, *That was when my parents took me to Washington, D.C.* "I went to the White House that year too," I said.

"I actually shook hands with President Coolidge," she said.

"I did too," I added. I was eleven years old at the time. I would never forget that.

"We had our picture taken in front of the White House," she said.

"So did we," I replied.

"Here I am," she said. My eyes followed her finger to a willowy schoolgirl. Then to my amazement I spotted the familiar face of a pudgy fifth-grader. I drew my finger beside Alma's and said, "Here *I* am, right next to you."

Joined in the photo before we had ever met, we were now married—and remained so for fifty-eight picture-perfect years.

—*Arthur Morgan*

❦

Comment

In every snapshot of our lives, the obvious and the hidden sit side by side, awaiting only the sharpening of our inner lens to reveal its deepest secrets.

I *stared* at our seven-month-old baby girl, Chelsea, in the hospital crib. As I tucked up her blanket, my eyes rested on the old Dillon family Bible I kept in the crib with her. It had belonged to my grandmother, who died when I was thirteen. I cherished that Bible as I had cherished my grandmother. She always soothed my childhood hurts and fears; to this day I still missed her. The Bible had rested in her hands during her funeral service. My mother removed it just before the coffin lid was lowered and later gave it to me.

But even Grandmother probably could not have soothed the hurt and fear my husband, Lance, and I now faced. Earlier that day the specialists at University Medical Center in Tucson had finally diagnosed the baffling condition that was slowly but surely draining the life from our first child.

"Chelsea has an extremely rare birth defect called severe combined immunodeficiency syndrome," our doctor informed us. "SCIDS interferes with the normal functioning of her immune system. She has virtually no natural defenses against infection. Her bone marrow doesn't produce the necessary cells."

I stood statue-still and stared at him. I remembered the movie *The Boy in the Plastic Bubble* about a child with the same condition. All along we'd hoped it was some obscure but defeatable bug causing the fever, diarrhea, and weight loss that ravaged Chelsea. I had prayed that somewhere in the mighty arsenal of modern medicine was the right drug, the magic bullet that would cure her. The immunologist carefully explained that the only option was a bone marrow transplant—a risky procedure that at best had about a fifty percent chance of success.

The *only* option.

We needed to transfer her to a hospital that did this sort of operation as soon as possible, he had said. There were only a few in the entire country.

Now as I stood over Chelsea's crib I smoothed the blanket and pushed the old Bible off to the side. Its leather cover was worn soft with use. As my child slept I closed my eyes and hoped for a miracle.

The next day we decided on Memorial Sloan-Kettering in Manhattan for the procedure because of their slightly-higher-than-average success rate. But now came the enormous problem of transporting Chelsea from Tucson to New York without exposing her to many people. Chelsea couldn't afford to catch even a cold. Any worsening in her condition would delay surgery. A simple flu bug could kill her.

Driving there was out of the question. She couldn't be off her IV fluids for that long. Commercial airliners posed too much hazard of contracting contagious disease, and big airports were even worse. We needed a private plane, but Chelsea's condition was not considered acutely critical—a criterion that had to be met before our insurance company would agree to cover the enormous cost of a jet. The catch-22 was that if Chelsea did become that critical, she would probably be too sick to have the surgery.

Lance and I were at wit's end. We didn't sleep, we barely ate. There had to be something we could do. We made countless phone calls. Finally we heard about a group called Corporate Angels, which provides free flights for sick children aboard private planes. The flights conduct normal business travel, and patients hitch along. Corporate Angels found us a flight leaving that Friday out of Denver bound nonstop for New York. A miracle was in our grasp.

"Dear God," I prayed, "now please help us get to Denver. I know You have Your ways. We'll just keep on trying."

Denver was too far to drive. We got the number of a private medevac company. Maybe we could pay for the flight ourselves. But when I talked to Judy Barrie, a paramedic whose husband, Jim, piloted the medevac plane, she gave me the bad news. "The flight will cost six thousand dollars, minimum," she said. We didn't have six thousand dollars. Our finances had been stretched to the limit.

I thanked Judy and said good-bye. "Wait," she said suddenly as I was about to hang up. "I really want to help you. I'm not promising anything, but I'll talk to Jim. Maybe he can figure this out."

When I hung up I had the strangest feeling that these people would be able to do something about what was increasingly a hopeless situation. An hour later Jim Barrie called back. "Listen, I've got a friend flying back an empty plane from Phoenix to Denver in the morning," Jim told me. "If you can get to the field by six-thirty, you can hitch along."

Perfect. Chelsea could handle the drive to Phoenix. But I was almost afraid to ask the next question. "Jim, what will it cost?"

"Cost? Heck, not a thing. This guy's a friend, and he's got to get his plane up there anyway."

I was faint with relief. These total strangers had taken a huge step in saving the life of my child. I didn't know what to say. The word *thanks* didn't seem big enough.

"You could do us one little favor, though," Jim added. "Judy and I would like to meet Chelsea."

Chelsea was awake and even a bit playful when Jim and Judy arrived at the hospital. While Jim talked to Lance about finding our way around the Phoenix airport, Judy and I chatted. Her eyes kept flitting over to the crib. Then I noticed she was staring at Grandma's Bible. One time when Judy was leaning over Chelsea, her fingers brushed it. Finally, as they were about to go, Judy asked, "Where are you from?" I told her Pittsburgh.

"I'm from Pittsburgh too," she said slowly. "Well, the suburb Carnegie actually."

"My mother is from Carnegie," I said. I felt a shiver go through me. "Virginia Everett. Dillon was her maiden name."

"Virginia Dillon?" Judy said, eyes wide. "My father was Howard Dillon."

"Uncle Howard?" I was stunned.

Judy nodded. It was as if a current of electricity had jumped between us. Now I could see why her face had seemed faintly familiar. Judy Barrie was my cousin Judy Dillon. "I haven't seen you since . . . ," I started to say. Judy's eyes jumped again to the Bible.

"Since Grandma's funeral twenty years ago," she finished the sentence. "That's the Bible she was holding."

We fell into each other's arms. I knew then that all would be well with Chelsea. The odds against this crossing of paths were simply too great. This was meant to be.

Chelsea got her bone marrow transplant and four months later she left the hospital with a healthy immune system. She is, as they say, a medical miracle.

And then there was that other miracle. I like to think of it as my grandmother's miracle. In a sense, even twenty years after her funeral, she was reaching out to comfort me and to assure me that with God all things are possible.

—*Cheryl Deep*

Comment
The power of love is no less potent than that of modern medicine. In the right hands, each serves as its own instrument of God's healing.

*L*ate in World War II my father was on the battlefront in Germany. In March 1945, while his Canadian regiment awaited supplies, Dad was ordered to Aldershot, England, to be decorated by King George VI.

The weather was raw in Aldershot, but Dad had given away his regulation greatcoat to a soldier back at the front. Shivering, he headed straight for the Red Cross center and picked from a bin full of sweaters a thick hand-knit one with a double collar. It fit perfectly under his tunic, warming him without breaking the uniform code.

After receiving the Military Medal for Bravery at Buckingham Palace, Dad rejoined the regiment and was issued another coat. He packed the sweater away in his kit.

Dad returned home safely to Canada in January 1946. His mother was glad to do his laundry again. While sorting his clothes, she held up the sweater, amazed. Then to my father's astonishment, she grabbed a pair of scissors and snipped the collar.

Like many women during the war, Grandma had knit sweaters for the young men overseas. She always put a note and postage money inside, so they could write back. "I prayed for the boys who would receive my handiwork, asking God to guide them safely home," she said. Many corresponded with her for years after.

While her hands had faithfully knitted, other Hands had guided her son safely home. Inside the collar of the sweater was some postage money—and a note she had written to a boy overseas.

—*Becky Alexander*

ଶ୍ରୁ

Comment

Kind fingers spread their warmth over cold oceans and distant continents to reach those who need a touch of home.

*N*igel Etherington of Wundowie, Australia, was driving down a highway one evening when he spotted an injured kangaroo, of the small variety known as a wallaby, lying motionless in the middle of the road—the victim, apparently, of a careless hit and run.

Overcome by the sight of the piteous creature, Nigel, an ardent animal lover, stopped his car to examine it. Having determined that it was still alive, Nigel scooped the two-and-a-half-foot-long male kangaroo into his arms, carried it into his car, and drove back to his farmhouse, where he proceeded to nurse it as best as he could.

"The next morning he seemed a bit better, but still groggy," Nigel remembers. "That night I placed him in the bathtub, leaving the door ajar, before going to bed."

A heavy sleeper, Nigel was rudely awakened around 7 A.M. by loud thumping noises. Muddled and dazed, he sat up in bed and immediately broke into spasms of coughing and choking. He could see nothing. Nigel suddenly realized that the reason his vision seemed impaired was because dense smoke was swirling all around him.

"We're on fire! Get out!" Nigel yelled as he raced down the hall to rouse a house guest.

As both made their escapes, Nigel saw a remarkable sight. The kangaroo was just inside the front door, furiously banging his heavy tail on the wooden floor and pounding desperately on the door with his front paws.

"Now I knew what woke me—and saved my life!" Nigel said. "I scooped him up under one arm, opened the door, and gasped my first lungfuls of fresh air."

Thirty-six hours after Nigel Etherington had saved the kangaroo's life, the kangaroo had returned the favor and saved his.

"The kangaroo saved him from being burned alive, there's no question about that," said Glenn Keeler, a spokesman for the Wundowie Fire Service in Australia.

In America, it's the dog who is man's best friend, but in Australia, it might very well be a . . . kangaroo.

I was attending social work school when I got the assignment that changed my life. The professor instructed that we write a fifteen-page paper on a client's case. He asked us to write about the case in minute detail. I felt stressed just thinking about it. Then he dropped the bomb. "Make Xerox copies of your paper to be given to each student in the class." My blood went cold.

I had written plenty of papers for school, but they were meant only for the teachers' eyes, never my peers. I had always harbored insecurities about my writing. And each paper I handed in, carried with it a barely tolerable degree of trepidation. But, this one really upped the ante. Now my writing would be laid open for all to see.

Every time I sat down to start the paper, my insecurities reigned supreme and my fingers promptly froze. I hadn't a clue about how to overcome this deadlock. An idea flashed in my head. "I'll get an editor!" Then my doubts kicked in. "But, where will I ever find an editor? And how can I possibly afford one?" Bereft of answers, I quickly ushered the fantasy out and made another attempt at getting back to work. Again, it failed. I welcomed the idea of somehow meeting an editor back to my thoughts and to my surprise, it actually comforted me.

While conducting research for the paper at Manhattan's mammoth Fifth Avenue Library, I found myself stumped by a particular question concerning the case. I telephoned a classmate for assistance. I enumerated the points I had thus far come up with and explained how I planned to formulate those ideas. I realized that the classmate felt incapable of helping me out of my dilemma. I thanked her and hung up. Just then, an older, diminutive woman waiting near the phone looked up at me and said with a determined air of authority, "You are coming from the wrong angle."

"What?" I asked, perplexed and a little annoyed. "Were you just listening to my conversation?"

"It doesn't matter," she said. "You are definitely coming from the wrong angle."

I wasn't sure whether to be amused or intrigued. "Well where do you think I should be coming from?"

She went on to give me one of the greatest lessons on writing I had ever experienced. I could see she evidently knew how I should approach this paper.

"Where did you learn to write so well?" I asked.

"It's my job. I'm an editor."

She told me her name was Henrietta Yusem and she worked for what was then called Harcourt, a major publishing house. I couldn't believe my good fortune. A few hours prior, I had prayed for an editor and here I stood face-to-face with this kind and competent woman, who was more than willing to provide me with what I needed—her masterful writing expertise. Still positioned in front of the library pay phone, Henrietta provided me with the perfect angle for my paper.

"Now go write!" she half scolded me, as though she knew me all my life.

"Can we meet again so that you can review it and edit it?" I asked, hoping against hope.

"Of course," she smiled.

We decided where and when to meet and that was how my magical friendship with Henrietta began.

At the time, I lived on the Upper West Side. Henrietta lived just a few blocks away. She kept her promise and came to edit my paper. She told me that her price would be my commitment to do the best job I was capable of doing. On the day of our second meeting, I handed her my fifteen-page paper with a significant amount of anxiety. I sat down opposite her so that I could catch her facial expressions as she read my paper. She finally finished the piece, and I held my breath, suddenly wishing I had never given it to her.

"If I were grading you, I would give you an A+."

"What?" I exclaimed. "Do you really mean it?"

"Of course I mean it," she insisted. "This is excellent." A surge of confidence flowed like an electric current throughout my body. I thought that if Henrietta could believe in me, then I could too.

From that life-changing moment, my battle with school papers ended. I gleaned confidence from a magical encounter with a good-hearted stranger, who was a stranger no more. We became fast friends. In fact, Henrietta insisted that we stay in touch by writing letters.

Hers came brimming with wisdom. I welcomed her constant guidance and support. Sometimes she sent along photographs and poetry, always with a loving touch.

In an age inundated with technology, with answering machines, faxes, e-mail and the like, I had found a comforting reprieve amid the turmoil. I looked forward to those handwritten letters from my dear friend just blocks away. I saved each letter as I would a jewel, knowing that one day, these limited treasures would cease.

Henrietta spent the last year of her life in a nursing home. Preferring not to be seen in her feeble condition, she asked me not to visit. She wanted us to continue to write one another. In keeping with our tradition, Henrietta's brother, Sy, also wrote me letters. In one such letter he informed me that whenever he would visit his sister, he would read to her from my first published book, *Small Miracles*, and that it brought her immeasurable moments of happiness.

Henrietta was my first editor, sent to me from above. She gave me a priceless gift—the confidence to express myself in writing. Henrietta taught me that we can slow down life's dizzying velocity to a more human-friendly pace and that in a city where faces stream by in endless anonymity, we can manage to make a meaningful connection if we only try.

Henrietta passed away on November 12, 1998. I miss her. Henrietta, this one's for you.

—Judith Leventhal

It was the summer of 1959, Marsha Goldstein's tenth summer, and her first at Camp Cejwin. She turned to her counselor, Naomi, and said excitedly, "My family is coming up for visiting day! I hope my uncle Stan will come up too." Naomi acknowledged this seemingly banal bit of information with a polite smile.

Visiting day arrived and Stan Altschul, a tall, dashing young man, walked through the entrance of Camp Cejwin in Glen Hale and made his way to Marsha's bunk house. Naomi realized that this must be "The Uncle" Marsha had referred to earlier that week. She was surprised by his strikingly good looks.

He stood silently before Naomi, as if waiting for her to initiate conversation. He soon dropped his shy veneer and revealed a man of refined wit and intelligence. Naomi thought how strange it was that Stan, aged twenty-three, had traveled all this distance to visit his little ten-year-old niece at camp. It became obvious through his gentle manner that he was also a man of great warmth and concern.

Ever since that meeting, Naomi couldn't shake Stan from her thoughts. She felt unsure about how to broach the topic with her young camper, but she knew one thing. She wanted to arrange for a date with Stan as soon as she went back home.

She didn't have to wait very long. Marsha's mother, on her own accord, broke the ice. "My brother is a shy one," she said. "Is it alright with you if I have him call you for a date?"

"But of course!" Naomi bolted, unable to temper her eagerness.

The closing days of August signaled the end of the summer. Counselors and campers exchanged teary good-byes and steadfast promises to stay in touch. Naomi and Marsha embraced, holding their secret wish within each of their hearts.

During the entire bus ride home, Naomi thought about her parents and joyfully anticipated seeing them again. The reunion fulfilled all her expectations and all was well, at least for a day.

That following morning, Naomi's father went off to work and she and her mother stayed home enjoying relaxing moments together for the first time in eight weeks. Later that afternoon, while waiting for her brother, Stephen, to come home, Naomi heard the doorbell and ran to answer it. A police officer stood before her.

"Is your father Philip Cohen?" he asked.

"Yes," she responded.

"Does your father work in Manhattan?" he asked.

"Yes," Naomi said, growing more confused.

"I'm sorry, but I'm afraid we have some bad news to tell you," he said. "Your father had a fatal heart attack." Overcome with shock, Naomi stood frozen in place.

She sat down and dropped her head, sobbing. The phone ring momentarily jolted her out of her grief. "Naomi?" came the familiar voice. It was Stan. Naomi managed to summon up enough strength to respond.

Through hot tears she said, "It's my father. My father passed away!"

After a painful pause, Stan broke the silence. Naomi had trouble focusing on his words, but found herself calmed by the genuine kindness in his voice.

Throughout that week many people stopped by to pay their condolences. One of them was Stan. His extraordinary sensitivity made a striking impact on Naomi. He barely knew her, yet made it his business to pay his respects.

Over the next many months, Stan helped Naomi heal from her great loss and over time the two fell in love and married. Naomi thought back to that fateful day in August when she lost her beloved father—the man she had loved from the very beginning of her days. Moments after hearing the tragic news, seeds were planted for a new tomorrow with a phone call from the man who would accompany her until the end of her days.

On the evening of February 28, 1996, Shafeeq Murrell bounded out the door of his South Philadelphia home to meet some friends for basketball. Shafeeq was a fifteen-year-old kid with a dazzling smile and a maturity far beyond his years. Popular with his peers, praised by his teachers, loving to his family, Shafeeq was the kind of son every mother dreams of having. On the way to his basketball game, Shafeeq met a couple of friends and stopped to talk.

Out of nowhere, two rival gangs opened fire. They blasted away at each other, warring for turf in a scene later described as "worse than the Wild West." Caught in the crossfire, Shafeeq Murrell tumbled to the ground.

His devastated family gathered at Children's Hospital. They cried and prayed and held each other tight as they gazed at his young body hooked up to life support. His older sister, Stacey, desperately wanted to believe that any minute, Shafeeq would rise up and give them all a hug. But as a nurse, she knew that was not possible. She steeled herself to talk to her parents about donating Shafeeq's organs.

At Temple Hospital in Philadelphia, Larry Montgomery, a thirty-nine-year-old dentist and father of three, lay hooked up to an IV, waiting for a heart. The past year had been a nightmare for Larry. All his life, he had been strong and athletic, with enough endurance to compete as a long-distance runner. But in March 1995 while jogging near his suburban home, he had stopped at the bottom of a hill, unable to scale it. A follow-up X-ray had revealed terrifying news: Larry was in complete heart failure.

The following months were a blur of one medical crisis after another, as Larry's condition rapidly deteriorated. By November, he was in the hospital hooked up to an IV, unable to do anything but wait for a donated heart. After three months in the hospital with no sign of a heart, however, Larry seemed condemned to go to an early grave, leaving his three young sons fatherless.

But on March 2, 1996, he was awakened with good news. His lucky break had come at last. At 3 o'clock in the morning, Larry Montgomery finally received a new heart.

The aftermath of his heart transplant was extraordinarily difficult. His body went into shock as it struggled to adjust to the strange new organ beating within it, and Larry lost consciousness for days.

He had no awareness of his family standing vigil by his bedside. He did not see the parade of doctors and nurses hovering over him, tending to his every need. He had no chance to wonder whose heart was now keeping him alive.

But his brother, Robert, did. A central, iron-clad principle of organ donation is that the donor remains anonymous. Most doctors believe that it is distracting, and even harmful, for someone with a transplanted organ to know the identity of his donor. But thanks to an odd set of circumstances, Robert began to suspect whose heart his brother now had.

By a strange twist, a video journalist was filming a documentary about transplants and covering Larry's case. The journalist saw the anguish of Larry's family as they waited for his recovery and took Robert aside.

"Don't worry," the journalist told Robert. "Your brother got a good heart, a young heart. Only fifteen years old."

Fifteen years old. . . . Robert took note of that fact. And he remembered it later that day, as he read in the newspaper about the violent death of a promising fifteen-year-old South Philadelphia boy. To Robert, the connection seemed too obvious to ignore.

When Larry finally emerged from unconsciousness, Robert handed him an envelope. "Someday when you feel up to it, you may want to read these," he said quietly. Inside the envelope was a pile of articles about Shafeeq Murrell.

Slowly, Larry recovered. He returned to his two-story colonial home in the suburbs and rebuilt his strength. He could no longer practice dentistry, because the medication created a tremor in his hands. But he lined up work as a teacher at the University of Pennsylvania Dental School and cautiously re-entered life.

Often his mind would wander to the family of Shafeeq Murrell. As he delighted in his three young sons and thanked God that he was alive to enjoy them he would think of the Murrell family and the young son they had loved so much and lost. The smooth, steady rhythm in his chest was a constant reminder of their pain. Sometimes, he felt overwhelmed by a desire to meet the Murrells and thank them face to face. He wanted them to know how blessed he felt that at their moment of deepest tragedy, they had chosen to grant him the gift of life.

But the knowledge that his happiness was mixed with their pain made Larry hesitant to contact them. Besides, life was busy with work and family and the constant struggle to maintain his health. Two years went by, and Larry still had not arranged to meet the Murrells.

On a Tuesday morning in the spring of 1998, Larry pulled into the parking lot at work and, as usual, joked with the parking attendant about his car. Larry drove an old Cadillac and the parking attendant, Mason Burnett, made no secret of his admiration for it.

"Dr. Montgomery, if you ever decide to sell this car, remember I'm your man," Mason told him, as he always did.

"Well, today's your lucky day," Larry said. "I just bought a new car. Give me a fair price and she's yours."

The two men agreed on a price and arranged to meet during lunch hour on Thursday. At the appointed hour, Larry arrived at the parking lot and Mason proposed that they drive to his house to get the money. Larry climbed into the passenger seat, Mason took the wheel, and the two men drove off together.

Larry grew increasingly uncomfortable as he realized Mason was driving them through the streets of South Philadelphia. The gloomy rain only added to his uneasiness. This was not his kind of neighborhood. These were not streets he ever wanted to know. Somewhere near here, the boy whose heart now beat in his chest had lived and died.

As Mason drove past Wharton Street, Larry felt a chill. "Mason, you know I have a heart transplant, right?" he said. "Well, I think my donor lived on that street we just passed."

"How did he die?" Mason asked.

"Some drug dealers were shooting at each other, and he got caught in the middle," said Larry.

To Larry's amazement, Mason burst into tears. "Shafeeq! Shafeeq!" he cried. "I was with him in intensive care. I was at his funeral. He worked with my wife every day."

He pulled over to the side of the road, too overcome to continue. "Would you do me a favor?" he said at last. "Call my wife, Ingrid. Tell her the story."

The rain was pouring down as Larry dashed to a pay phone. "Ingrid? This is Larry Montgomery. I'm the one who's selling you the car."

"Nice to meet you," Ingrid said pleasantly.

"Yeah. And I think I have Shafeeq Murrell's heart."

"Oh my God!" Ingrid shrieked. "I'm looking at his picture right now! It's right on my desk! He was the finest boy I ever knew."

She proceeded to tell him about Shafeeq. He had been assigned as a volunteer summer intern at the city housing agency where she worked. But he had done such an outstanding job that the agency had taken the highly unusual step of putting him on the permanent payroll.

Everyone in the office had loved Shafeeq. He was polite, helpful, and intensely worried about everyone else's safety. Each night after work, he had walked Ingrid to the subway to make sure she was all right. The one exception was that terrible day in February when he left work a little early to pick up his gym bag before basketball.

"Let me tell you something, Mr. Montgomery," said Ingrid with a sob. "That's a good, kind heart you've got in there."

Larry brooded for days about the incredible coincidence he had just experienced. He was a suburban dentist for whom inner-city Philadelphia was such a foreign world it might as well have been Australia. Yet, almost as if by magic, he had been delivered straight into Shafeeq's neighborhood and directly connected to his life. It was so strange, so fantastic, so utterly unexpected.

Till now, Shafeeq had been an abstraction to Larry. Now he seemed very real. He picked up the phone and arranged to meet Shafeeq's family.

The meeting took place in the office of the Delaware Valley Transplant Program, which had coordinated the donation of Shafeeq's heart.

Larry brought his wife, Sheree, and his three sons, ages thirteen, eleven, and nine. They were led into a private room. The door opened. In walked Shafeeq's mother, Gail, and his father, Clarence. Shafeeq's older sister, Stacey, followed with his grandmother, aunt, and cousins. But Shafeeq's younger brother and sister could not bring themselves to meet the man with their brother's heart. They stayed home.

The meeting was emotional. Gail looked at Larry, at his wife and children. Her eyes grew misty. "What a beautiful family you have," she told Larry. "One thing is clear to me. The heart has no color."

Larry's wife, Sheree, struggled to put into words all her powerful feelings. She thanked Gail and Clarence from the bottom of her heart for giving Larry the gift of life. She told them how grateful she was for every single day, every single hour that Larry had been granted, and how much it meant to her children to have their father. She spoke, too, about how deeply her family felt the loss of the Murrell family.

Gail and Clarence talked about what a fine young man their son had been. They spoke with pride of his plans to help his community when he grew up. And they showed the Montgomerys a tribute that they had created: a T-shirt with a picture of Shafeeq and underneath it the inscription, *"What's loved is never lost."*

Shafeeq's sister, Stacey, asked to speak privately to Larry. They stepped into the hall. Stacey leaned her head against Larry's chest and silently listened to his heart.

Then she said, "I haven't been able to bring myself to go to the cemetery. Maybe now I can."

After that initial meeting, the Mongomerys and the Murrells stayed frequently in touch. They were friendly, but somehow they were more than friends. Their relationship was warm, affectionate, and filled with deep mutual respect. Larry began to regard the Murrells as a kind of extension of his own family.

In January of 1999, Gail called Larry with the big news: the trial of Shafeeq's alleged murderers was about to begin. Larry didn't hesitate for a minute. He knew where he had to be.

On a snowy Friday morning, Larry Montgomery sat next to Gail Murrell, watching two young men being led into a Philadelphia courtroom. The moment was so intense that he felt faint. Everything was coming together into one room . . . These men had pulled a trigger and with that single action, had destroyed Shafeeq's life and saved his own. His heart—Shafeeq's heart—pounded wildly in his chest.

Throughout the trial, Larry stayed by the Murrells' side. When the coroner took the stand and described

Shafeeq's fatal wound, Larry put his hand on Gail's hand. When the coroner said that Shafeeq's mother and father had been kind enough to donate his organs, Larry and the Murrells exchanged tearful smiles. And when the prosecution showed a video in which the defendants confessed, Larry sat stolidly by the Murrells' side, trying to offer strength and support.

Neither Larry or the Murrells took any joy in the guilty verdict or in the resulting sentence of life imprisonment. There was too much pain in the eyes of the murderers' families for them to feel triumph. Instead, Larry wrestled with overwhelming feelings of guilt.

"I looked around the courtroom and all I saw was tragedy," he told the Murrells. "Your family. The family of those boys who'll be in jail for life. I'm the only one who got something good out of this."

"Don't feel that way," Stacey Murrell told Larry. "We're just glad you're alive."

Stacey's response, so typical of the generous spirit of the Murrell family, filled Larry's heart. Once again, for the hundredth time, he pondered the incredible coincidence that had brought them together. If he had not sold his car to their friend, he may never have wandered into their neighborhood and their lives. It was that coincidence that had inspired him with the belief that he was part of some mysterious plan—a plan that demanded that he meet the Murrells.

But what was the plan? Maybe, in the aftermath of the trial, he finally understood. He could never repay the Murrells the debt that he owed them. But maybe, just maybe, he could bring them a little consolation. He was more than their friend. He was a living legacy of their love. Whenever he was near, Shafeeq was near, too. And maybe, with God's help, they could find some solace in that.

"You know, Larry," Gail Murrell said one day. "We gave away all of Shafeeq's organs. Nobody else ever tried to contact us. But that's okay. Because the one person that we all hoped and prayed would try to find us was the person with Shafeeq's heart."

—Peggy Sarlin

❧

Comment

After the trial was over, Larry delivered a gift to the Murrell home. It was a beautiful jewelry box. On the top shone a golden heart, in which Larry had engraved, *"What's loved is never lost."*

*M*y eighty-eight-year-old mother-in-law, who stands all of 4 feet 10 inches and weighs 80 pounds, has a habit of carrying an old supermarket sack with her whenever we go anywhere. This is in addition to her large handbag. So on her birthday, I decided it would be a lot better if she had a small tote bag in which to carry her extra stuff. Somehow the days got away from me and I found myself running from store to store on her birthday looking for what I thought would be an easy to find purchase. To my dismay, I discovered that small tote bags are almost nonexistent!

My last stop was a local bookstore as I had an appointment and knew that if I didn't find a tote bag there, I would have to abandon the whole idea. After searching through the store and seeing no tote bags, I started for the door when a book caught my eye entitled *Small Miracles*. I grabbed the book and got in line at the cashier's. After he rung up the sale, you can imagine my astonishment when he pulled out a small tote bag from behind the counter and announced that it was free with the purchase of the book!

The message on the bag?

"I believe in Small Miracles."

—*Kathleen Rosenau*

Acknowledgments

Our thanks go first and foremost to YOU, our cherished readers, whose enthusiasm for the message of our books has been boundless and immensely gratifying. Because of your warmth and excitement—translated into 800,000 copies sold so far—we have been able to proceed with the third book, and, hopefully even more in the near future. We have been enormously moved by your kind and sincere letters and are very heartened to know that *Small Miracles* has brought you joy and comfort. You our readers are the co-creators of this sequel, and we applaud you for your open hearts and contagious excitement. Thank you.

Our deep gratitude also goes to everyone at Adams Media Corporation, who launched this series with so much trust, belief, and devotion. We feel privileged to be working with such special and talented people. To the extraordinary Bob Adams, who took such enormous personal interest in the fate of this small book and expended so much creative energy in launching it, and who believed in the book even more after he experienced his own first "small miracle" the very night he finished reading the galleys—thank you for everything. To Wayne Jackson, innovative and dynamic Director of Marketing whose zeal for the book was contagious and set booksellers on fire—thank you. To the wonderful women in the publicity department—Carrie, Rachel and Michelle— thank you! Carrie Lewis, Publicity Director, deserves special kudos for her outstanding work. Linda Spencer does a fantastic job as Managing Editor. Thank you, Linda.

We have been blessed with the most wonderful editor, Pamela Liflander, whose expert advice, gentle wisdom, and intelligent counsel has greatly enriched our writing experience. We have concluded that Pam, whose patience and good humor has proven unflagging over three years of interaction, basically borders near sainthood, and we have been the happy beneficiaries of this paragon's enormous range of estimable virtues. Thank you, Pam! We also want to acknowledge the exceptional efforts of copyeditor extraordinaire Virginia Ruebens, who performs magic with our prose. Thank you, Virginia.

During this momentous year in our life, we have been privileged to meet many wonderful booksellers who believed in our book and handsold it magnificently. We are grateful to all of you, too numerous to mention here, and we applaud your efforts. There are three independent stores, however, that deserve special mention. No store has championed *Small Miracles* more fervently than Harnik's Happy House in Brooklyn. Noreen Harnik and Terri Roca and their devoted staff — Minnie, Frances and Rose — threw such incredible support behind *Small Miracles* that they have made it into the number one all-time best-selling book in their store's fifty-year history. We will forever be indebted to them for their tremendous generosity of heart and magnanimity of spirit. Thank you, everyone at Harnik's.

We also want to mention two very special stores — Eichlers of Boro Park and Eichlers of Flatbush — that have been incredibly supportive of our books in a very big way. The staff is the greatest, and we are very appreciative of their support and advocacy. Thanks to Moish Perl, Yossi Pearson, Cheski Blau, and Meryl Scheller. Special appreciation is warmly extended to two outstanding staff members—Aryeh Goldberger and Yitzi Rosenblum—for exceptional efforts and kindness. They have really gone out on a limb for us. Edna Krausz of Inspiration Gallery in New Rochelle, New York, we thank you.

We are both members of an informal women's group, which stresses spirituality and creative living, and we want to thank the very special members of the group for their ongoing support and genuine sharing in our success. Thank you Pesi, Etta, Ruchama, Miriam, and Shulamis! We look forward to many years together! We extend our deepest gratitude, love and appreciation to Ruth Wolfert for enriching us with her wisdom and insight.

Finally, we would also like to thank our agent, Richard Pine, for his guidance and support.

Yitta would like to thank her colleagues at EMUNAH for their gracious support always and for overlooking many conspicuous absences over the year as a result of both book tour and book writing commitments.

When I was a little girl and just beginning to write, I had a great friend and advocate in Irene Klass, owner and editor of *The Jewish Press*. Her encouragement of my puerile writing efforts was pivotal in my life, and I am indebted to her forever. The torch has now been passed to her daughter, Naomi Mauer, who has also become a special person in my life. Thank you, Naomi, for your steadfast friendship and constant support. And great appreciation also to Sheila Abrams, for your wonderful kindnesses all these years.

The greatest moments in life are the ones shared by friends and family. The enthusiasm and support demonstrated by my dear friends—Raizy Steg, Bella Friedman, Annette

Grauman, Babshi Chanowitz, Sarah Laya Landau, Hindy Rosenberg and Fanny Mitchell—are very precious to me. Anna Ashton, my devoted assistant, deserves tremendous applause for her outstanding devotion and wonderful assistance in every phase of my life. I love you, Anna!

Special thanks also to Ginny Duffy for holding my hand when I most needed it. When the going got tough, I got going to one of these two mentors. Thanks to Chris Santerra of *Synchronicity Times* for posting my request for stories on her Web site. Also, warmest gratitude to Rabbi Meir Fund, my Rabbi, counselor, and guide who creates miracles every day! And to the brilliant, talented, and generous-hearted Georgie, who is always there and always has been there—I love you!

Bill and Lili Cunningham have become new and precious friends over the past year, and I cherish and treasure the immense riches with which they have gifted me. Not only is Bill a wonderful friend, but a wonderful writer as well, and his two stories have enhanced this book in a big way. Peggy Sarlin, whom I have always adored, has reentered my life and come aboard as a contributor to *Small Miracles*. Her talent is awesome to behold.

My family—my mother, Claire Halberstam; my brother, Moishe Halberstam; and my sister, Miriam Halberstam, have supported my efforts faithfully as have my in-laws, Leib and Sima Mandelbaum, Suri and Danny Dymshits, Chaim and Bayla Mandelbaum, Yeruchem and Chaya Winkler. My sister, Miriam, continuously scours through myriad newspapers, magazines, and books and watches an endless stream of television talk shows in the hope of finding some "small miracle" nugget recounted on the broadcast media.

Several of the stories published in this book emanated from her dedicated efforts, and I cannot thank her enough.

My two children—Yossi and Eli—have been joyous participants in the whole wonderful, exciting process and very indulgent of my deficiencies as a mother throughout. They have graciously forgiven me my flaws and absences during this hectic period.

My husband, Motty, is actually responsible—more than anybody else—in nurturing my creativity during adulthood. (My father of blessed memory was the primary source during childhood.) Throughout the twenty-two years of our marriage, Motty has always insisted, sincerely and with genuine devotion, that I eschew the kitchen in favor of the computer, and he has always reveled in my successes as if they were his own. His wisdom and counsel have helped me on dozens of occasions, and his feedback and input have proven pivotal. More than anything else, living with him and being exposed to his brilliant insights and original way of thinking has helped me grow as a human being. And for that, I owe him a tremendous debt.

— *Yitta Halberstam*

I thank Jules, my dear beloved husband who continues to be my partner in every respect of the word. He has shown me how to face my perceived limitations, challenge them and move beyond. I am deeply grateful for his unwavering support in my endeavors.

I want to acknowledge my two little girls, Arielle and Shira, who continuously remind me of the true meaning of "small miracles." Their vibrant energy is contagious and it has helped to fuel my enthusiasm for writing this sequel.

Estee, my sister, friend, and confidant has been a blessing in my life since the moment she was born. My dear mother, Rose, and Hedy and Myer Feiler and children, Isser and Malku Handler, Anne Leventhal, Emery, David and Shulamit Leventhal and children have all provided a loving and supportive family.

Much gratitude is also extended to Pesi Dinnerstein who is my beacon of light. Sara Barris, Deena Edleman, Ruchama and Yisrael Feurerman, and Eta Ansel have been close friends who have been so generous with their enthusiasm. Elli Wohlgelernter is a dear friend and has loved coincidences all his life. I want to acknowledge Jonathan and Ruchy Mark who have, through their words, reflected back to us the beauty of our book and together, they have been the catalyst for many miracles.

Along the book tour, I have met numerous people who have made the tour an exciting and wonderful experience. In particular, I want to thank Elaine Stundell, Tony Gangi, Irene Polemis and their respective co-workers of Barnes and Noble, for their graciousness, generosity, and enthusiasm for the book.

And lastly, I want to acknowledge Yitta, my co-author, my "soul-sister," my dear friend. Yitta lives by the principles of this book. Her sincere concern and empathy for people is woven into the fabric of her writing and it is at the heart of the magic of this book. When we signed our first book contract, a gentleman remarked, "Well, there goes the friendship." Well, he was wrong. With a partner like Yitta, every day I learn more about the true meaning of love and friendship. . . . a priceless gift of *Small Miracles*.

—*Judith Leventhal*

Permissions

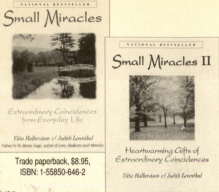